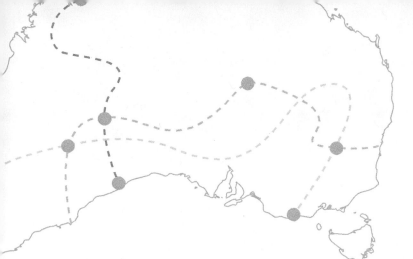

P9-DWT-989

Double N Adventures

A Complete Office Simulation

Double N Adventures

A Complete Office Simulation

Roxane L. Rowsell

College of the North Atlantic

NELSON

Double N Adventures:
A Complete Office Simulation

by Roxane Rowsell

Vice President,
Editorial Director:
Evelyn Veitch

Editor-in-Chief,
Higher Education:
Anne Williams

Acquisitions Editor:
Maya Castle

Marketing Manager:
Kathaleen McCormick

Developmental Editor:
Elke Price

Photo Researcher:
Debbie Yea

Permissions Coordinator:
Debbie Yea

Content Production Manager:
Christine Gilbert

Copy Editor:
Matthew Kudelka

Proofreader:
Dawn Hunter

Production Coordinator:
Ferial Suleman

Design Director:
Ken Phipps

Managing Designer:
Franca Amore

Interior Design:
Sharon Lucas

Interior Image:
background of chapter opener:
Jerry Kobalenko/Getty Images

Cover Design:
Carianne Sherriff

Cover Image:
©Henri Georgi/All Canada Photos

Compositor:
Tammy Gay

COPYRIGHT © 2011 by Nelson Education Ltd.

Printed and bound in Canada
6 7 8 9 20 19 18 17

For more information contact Nelson Education Ltd., 1120 Birchmount Road, Toronto, Ontario, M1K 5G4. Or you can visit our Internet site at nelson.com

ALL RIGHTS RESERVED. No part of this work covered by the copyright herein may be reproduced, transcribed, or used in any form or by any means—graphic, electronic, or mechanical, including photocopying, recording, taping, Web distribution, or information storage and retrieval systems—without the written permission of the publisher.

For permission to use material from this text or product, submit all requests online at cengage.com/permissions. Further questions about permissions can be emailed to permissionrequest@cengage.com

Every effort has been made to trace ownership of all copyrighted material and to secure permission from copyright holders. In the event of any question arising as to the use of any material, we will be pleased to make the necessary corrections in future printings.

Library and Archives Canada Cataloguing in Publication

Rowsell, Roxane, 1974-

Double n adventures : a complete office simulation / Roxane Rowsell.

ISBN 978-0-17-650209-6

1. Office management--Study and teaching--Simulation methods.

I. Title.

HF5547.5.R693 2010
651.3'078
C2010-902941-0

ISBN-10: 0-17-650209-2
ISBN-13: 978-0-17-650209-6

CONTENTS

v

Contents

PREFACE

To The Instructor

Double N Adventures is designed to be a "capstone experience" in a complete simulated office environment. Your students are the administrative assistant for Double N Adventures, an adventure tourism company based in Newfoundland. The purpose of this book is to allow the students to complete their administrative duties independently, with little or no supervision. They will be expected to apply what they have learned in previous administration courses to this course. Students should have already acquired some proficiency in Microsoft Word 2007, Microsoft Excel 2007, Microsoft PowerPoint 2007, Microsoft Access 2007 (optional), Microsoft Outlook 2007, and with Internet browsing software before beginning this course.

The *Company Policies and Procedures* section contains all the information your students require regarding Double N Adventures, its policies, and the procedures needed for completing various tasks. Chapters 1 through 5 collectively represent a workweek and each of these chapters contains various jobs and tasks to make up a full workday in an office environment. Although the completion time for this course will vary depending on the students' skill level, the text provides approximately 40 hours of work.

Instructor's Resources

An Instructor's Manual and Answer Key are available as a downloadable supplement on the book's companion website at http://www.doublenadventures.com. The Instructor's Manual contains teaching notes, a list of tasks for each chapter, and some teaching suggestions for each task. Solutions for all jobs are provided in the Answer Key which can be used in evaluating student work or for demonstrating a sample solution. A grading rubric is also provided to assist you when marking the student's work. For some of the jobs that require students to prepare brochures, conduct Internet research, or format or make content decisions, the Answer Key provides examples of completed jobs.

Companion Website

The book's companion website, http://www.doublenadventures.com, contains the data, image, and audio files that students require in order to complete the various tasks and jobs in the book. These files, such as emails, documents, or templates are organized by days of the week. The audio file icons that appear in the book's margins alert the student that they must listen to the audio files to complete that job.

Acknowledgments

There are many people that I would like to thank for making this project a reality. I would especially like to thank the Office Administration instructors across Canada who work tirelessly to ensure that the Office Administration students are graduating with the skills and education they need to enter into the ever-changing and ever-evolving office administration field. It is with you in mind that I created a text that will challenge students and bridge the distance between student and employee. Many thanks to all the Office Administration students who will accept this text as a stepping stone to their careers and will take on the challenge without reservations. Developing a textbook that will help you be successful was my ultimate goal.

For their useful suggestions and valuable insight that helped to shape this first edition, I am grateful to the reviewers, who took time out of their busy schedules to review the proposal and manuscript. All of your suggestions were carefully reviewed and I worked diligently to implement as many of your ideas as I could. Hats off to Susan Byrne at St. Clair College; Thomas Dawson at Eastern College; Dawn Devonshire at Saskatoon Business College; Christine Doody at Algonquin College; Julie Magerka at Centennial College; Sylvia Ranson at Conestoga College; Alice Szrajber at Mohawk College; and Kelly Taylor-Hulan at College of the North Atlantic. I would like to offer a special word of appreciation for the understanding and tremendous support of my colleague and friend Kelly Taylor-Hulan, who was my sounding board and confidant throughout this process.

I am also grateful to the team at Nelson Education, who have been nothing less than amazing. Anne Williams, thank you for sharing my vision and for all your guidance and support. Elke Price, thank you for holding my hand through this entire process; you have been patient, supportive, and a pleasure to work with. I appreciate the guidance you have shown this first-time author. Many thanks Christine Gilbert, content production manager, Matthew Kudelka, copy editor, and Dawn Hunter, proofreader.

Although the vision for this book may have been mine, I can assure you that it would not have happened without the support of my family and friends. A special thank you to my husband, Tim, my parents, and of course my inspiration, my twin boys, Nicolas and Noah.

Roxane Rowsell
August, 2010

Source: Simon Krzic/Shutterstock

Introduction

Welcome to *Double N Adventures: A Complete Office Simulation*. This book is designed to challenge you in a hands-on simulated office environment. You are the administrative assistant for this outdoor adventure company. Throughout the text, you will learn about how the company operates and be asked to do many tasks and jobs. In this section, you will find the information you will need to succeed.

This text is designed to be a "capstone experience"—that is, you will be expected to apply all that you have learned in previous courses to this course. You will be expected to

- make decisions;
- use good judgment;
- act professionally;
- take responsibility;
- be proactive;
- show initiative;
- be a problem solver;
- create documents from minimal information;
- use research skills; *and*
- follow the rules for creating business documents.

As you work through the many jobs and tasks in this text, you will be making most of the decisions. As in real life, you will be responsible for ensuring that the work is done in a professional and timely manner. When typical office problems and conflicts occur, you will have to use good judgment to find solutions. Working through the situations and tasks in this text will prepare you to become a successful administrative assistant.

Text Contents

The information in this text is arranged as follows:

- The **Introduction** outlines what will be expected from you for you to successfully complete the requirements of this text.

- The **Company Policies and Procedures** section contains all the information you will need regarding Double N Adventures, its policies, and the procedures for completing various tasks.

- **Chapters 1 through 5** collectively represent a workweek. Each chapter contains various jobs and tasks that would make up a full workday in an office.

- **Appendix A: Working Papers** provides sample documents, including letters, memos, reports, and invoices. Electronic versions of all the documents found in this appendix are available on the book's companion resource site at http://www.doublenadventures. nelson.com.

- **Appendix B: Client Database** provides a list of the company's clients. The electronic file is available on the book's companion resource site at http://www.doublenadventures. nelson.com.

Prerequisites for This Course

To succeed as the administrative assistant for Double N Adventures, you should have already acquired skills in the following software programs:

- Microsoft Word 2007

- Microsoft Excel 2007

- Microsoft PowerPoint 2007

- Microsoft Access 2007 (optional)

- Microsoft Outlook 2007

- A Web-browsing application, such as, but not limited to, Microsoft Internet Explorer

Source: Stan Cook/Stan Cook Sea Kayaking Adventures

Double N Adventures

Double N Adventures was started four years ago by two brothers, Nick and Noah Rockwell, who had been avid adventure seekers for several years. Both graduated from an adventure tourism program at their local college. They are constantly taking on new challenges and experiences that push their limits. Because of this, they have earned a reputation for being leaders in their field and for delivering safe and exciting adventure experiences in Newfoundland. Examples of the types of adventure bookings that Double N Adventures offers include white-water rafting, backcountry caving, deep-sea fishing, canoeing, kayaking, and hiking.

The Staff

Management

Though Nick and Noah have passion, drive, and business experience, they would rather be outside enjoying the hands-on portion of the business. They've hired Georgia K. Taylor, who has managed canoeing and kayaking trips and events throughout Canada. Georgia is a bright, young businesswoman who has new ideas, endless enthusiasm, and a desire to make Double N Adventures the best adventure company anywhere. She is strong-willed, focused, and stern. Her approach to doing business is very different from Nick and Noah's, and you can expect that these differences will bring a unique set of adventures.

Adventure Guides

Double N Adventures also employs four adventure guides, who are responsible for conducting the tours: Paul Makin, Rebecca Chance, Kelly Tanner, and Tim Reegan. All are licensed guides and guide instructors. They have worked for various adventure businesses and have more than 30 years of combined experience. Their job is to provide safe, exciting experiences for their clients.

Source: Kelly Taylor-Hulan

Administrative Assistant

You are the administrative assistant of Double N Adventures. You have three supervisors or bosses: Nick Rockwell, Noah Rockwell, and Georgia Taylor. As administrative assistant, you will sometimes have to prioritize and handle conflicting information. For example, you may be given two different dates for the same meeting. You will have to follow up on this information and find the most professional way to proceed. Remember, *you* have to check the work, *you* have to check the dates, and *you* have to check the information in the documents you produce.

Job Description

As the administrative assistant for Double N Adventures, you will be expected to carry out many tasks. Some of these include

- maintaining booking schedules for all adventures, staff, and equipment;
- setting up meetings, booking the boardroom, creating and distributing agendas, and ordering break or lunch items;
- ordering supplies;
- sending out invoices;
- maintaining and updating the clientele database;
- maintaining a vendor list;
- creating promotional materials;
- creating office documents;
- submitting payroll information for the adventure guides on Fridays;
- coordinating events among three supervisors and that ensuring each supervisor has the same information;
- researching information on the Internet;
- preparing presentations by using PowerPoint;
- providing support to the adventure guides;
- making hotel and flight reservations;
- maintaining a to-do list;
- completing deposit forms;
- maintaining office records;
- scheduling maintenance for adventure equipment;
- creating documents from handwritten notes;
- processing incoming mail and e-mails;
- answering incoming telephone calls;
- maintaining a professional composure at all times;
- maintaining a professional working environment and company image; *and*
- being positive.

The Art of Being Positive

There is nothing easier than being critical and knocking down others' ideas. It's a bit more difficult to come up with a possible solution and win allies to implement it. So, it's no wonder that the world is full of pessimists when what we really need is more creative, far-sighted, optimistic, well-positioned risk takers. What can you do to join the category of realistic optimists and better your chances of being perceived as a leader, a visionary, and a promotable team member?

- Recognize that repeated negative input gets you attention for the moment— but also labels you as a group misfit and lessens the respect that fellow group members have for you.

- If you have legitimate concerns, voice them before the group adopts an action. Once the group has decided to move ahead on a path, support the decision and move forward.

- Don't just shoot ideas down; offer constructive and doable alternatives.

- If you consistently disagree with the group, maybe you need to find a new group that better fits with your personal ideology. Your continued negativism is a bummer for both you and the group.

- Don't run ideas through just your own personal and limited radar screen. Look for other successful models.

- Once you've voiced your disapproval, drop it. Nagging gets you nowhere and gives you a bad name.

- If you truly don't understand something, don't hold the group back with your wariness; instead, arrange for a private tutoring session with the person who proposed the solution.

- It is neither cute nor savvy to always be seen as the Doubting Thomas. Design a more professional image for yourself.

If you find that you are almost always in the minority or a naysayer, take a good look at yourself. You might need an attitude adjustment. This could be a symptom of something deeper that needs to be addressed. If you don't address it, you could be inadvertently holding yourself back from future personal and professional success.

Source: International Association of Administrative Professionals, http://www.iaap-hq.org.

5

Introduction

Evaluation

You will be evaluated upon the completion of each chapter. In each chapter, you will be asked to do a variety of jobs, produce many documents, make arrangements for meetings, book appointments, and so on. Your instructor will grade each chapter as a whole package. Each job or task will be assigned a points value, and every portion of that job will be graded by using a rubric specific to each job.

A sample grading rubric is provided below. (NOTE: This isn't the actual rubric that your instructor will be using.) As you can see, it is important that you pay attention to detail and proofread your work for errors and omissions.

Sample Grading Rubric
Task: Merge Letter Form Document

Description of Job	Points	Your Score
A form letter was created	10	
Letterhead with logo was used	5	
Correct contact name and address were included	2	
Proper spacing was used	5	
Date was included	2	
Body was well written	10	
Body included:		
Date of meeting	5	
Location of meeting	5	
Tour of facilities to follow	5	
Brochure enclosed	5	
Typos (subtract 2 points for each typo)	(0)	
Proper grammar (subtract 2 points for each grammar mistake)	(0)	
Student's initials	1	
Enclosure	5	
Total points	60	

The purpose of the rubric is to ensure grading consistency between students and to eliminate ambiguity in grading. All jobs are graded on the same number of points (for example, all *Merge Letter Form Documents* are worth 60 points, as illustrated above). Keeping a to-do list and maintaining the schedule (these documents are discussed in the Company Policies and Procedures section) are examples of jobs. Each job discussed in the chapter will be evaluated by using a grading rubric.

To further explain the grading process, the example below shows how a chapter may be graded:

- Chapter 1 may have eight jobs of varying difficulty that collectively are graded out of 320 points.

  > One job may be to create a letter. Each part of the letter would be evaluated individually. The letter may be worth a total of 60 points.

  > Another job may be to create an invitation for which you would be evaluated on your attention to detail and your creativity, as well as your ability to create a professional-looking document.

Tip Boxes

Each chapter contains tip boxes, which recap many of the skills you have learned or provide general information related to the job that may be helpful to you. They will not teach you new skills. Remember, this text is designed to offer a capstone experience, so you should already have a complete set of skills that you can pull from. Be resourceful! Use tools such as the Internet or the Help feature in the software program you're using when you are trying to complete a job. For example, if you can't remember how to merge documents, figure it out! At this point in your studies, you should be able to complete the tasks in this text without step-by-step instructions. Keep in mind that you may not know how to complete every job, but that doesn't mean you can't *find out* how to complete every one.

> **>tip**

It is in your best interest to read all of the tip boxes and follow the directions given.

Student Data Files and Website

You will need data files to complete the various tasks and jobs. These files are provided on the textbook's website at http://www.doublenadventures.nelson.com. There you will find e-mails, documents, templates, and correspondence files organized by the days of the week. The details of when to use each data file will be provided to you, but the steps to completing the related job will not be spelled out for you.

Additional activities appear in each chapter. They may be as simple as opening a document on the website to find out a new meeting time. Such tasks may seem small; however, your ability to cross-reference and complete these jobs will help your instructor evaluate your attention to detail—a valuable skill that many employers look for.

Audio Files

Audio file icons appear in the margins. These icons alert you that you must listen to an audio file to complete the job. The files are located on the book's website.

Go to
http://
www.doublenadventures.
nelson.com
to listen to an audio file.

Source: Joel Blit/Shutterstock

Let's Begin

You are now ready to begin this project. To complete each task correctly, you first must read the Company Policies and Procedures section. Once you've finished reading this section, you should refer to it often. Among other things, it can help you organize the list of jobs you will need to complete. Note that not all the tasks you must do are listed in the chapters. Some additional jobs will be required, and you must demonstrate foresight and attention to detail in order to identify and complete them. Chapters 1 through 5 represent a full workweek: Chapter 1 is Monday, Chapter 2 is Tuesday, and so on. Since each weekday in the text is based on a full workday's tasks, it should take you seven to eight hours to complete each chapter.

Good luck! You now have the opportunity to demonstrate that you have a comprehensive understanding of the software, document production, and office procedures you have learned and that you are therefore equipped to become a successful office administrator.

How to Be a Great Team Player

The ability to get along well with groups of individuals is not an easy task for some. Not all people have the ability to function well in a team setting, and some even find it quite difficult to do so. To become a good team player, you have to develop and hone certain traits (if you don't yet have them). The following five traits will help make you both an asset to any team and a person other people would enjoy working with to achieve common goals.

- **Be a good listener.** Project managers and team leaders are always on the lookout for people who can listen well so that they can feel confident that goals are clearly and well understood. Good team players also listen to and respect others' views, opinions, and strategies.

- **Show cooperation rather than competition.** Good team players don't compete with other members of their team but rather work with them to achieve a common goal. Not to say that competition is bad, but a great team player should be more concerned about achieving a team goal than about achieving his or her own individual goals.

- **Be adaptable and flexible.** Being flexible is important if you want to be a good team player. When working (or playing) with a team, you have to understand that you're dealing not with only a single person but rather with a group of diverse people. You should be ready to adapt to any person and to any situation.

- **Have a positive outlook.** To become a successful team player, you should be a person whom others love to be around. If you have a positive outlook on life and exude positive vibes, people normally will love to work or play alongside you, fostering a better environment for great teamwork.

- **Meet deadlines and do your part really well.** When working or playing on a team, understand that you are a part of a whole and that your part in the whole is crucial to the achievement of team goals.

To succeed at being a great team player, you have to see and understand the greater picture and be more concerned with achieving the team's goals than your own personal ones.

Source: Adapted from Olivia Cooper/HowToDoThings.com

Source: Sergey Kamshylin/Shutterstock

Company Policies and Procedures

In this section you will find the information you need in order to succeed in this course. It is up to you to read this information, record any vital points, and refer to it as often as necessary. Your instructor is not responsible for teaching you this information. Remember, this text simulates the workings of a *real office*, and in the real world, your instructor will not be there to guide you.

Company Information
Employees

Name	Position
Nick Rockwell	Co-owner, Part-Time Adventure Guide
Noah Rockwell	Co-owner, Part-Time Adventure Guide
Georgia Taylor	Office Manager
Paul Makin	Adventure Guide
Rebecca Chance	Adventure Guide
Kelly Tanner	Adventure Guide
Tim Reegan	Adventure Guide
You	Administrative Assistant

Company Slogan

Would You Like an Adventure Today?

Contact Information

Double N Adventures
93 Red Cliff Road
Treasure Bay, NL A9V 2K8
Phone Number: (709) 807-4214
Toll-Free Number: 1-877-807-4214
Fax Number: (709) 807-4215
http://www.doublenadventures.ca

E-mail Addresses

Office@doublenadventures.ca (This is your e-mail address.)

Nick@doublenadventures.ca

Noah@doublenadventures.ca

Georgia@doublenadventures.ca

Paul@doublenadventures.ca

Rebecca@doublenadventures.ca

Kelly@doublenadventures.ca

Tim@doublenadventures.ca

Office Hours

Monday to Friday, 8 a.m. to 5 p.m.

- Administrative assistant's hours of work: 8 a.m. to 5 p.m.
- Adventure guides' hours of work: 7 a.m. to 6 p.m.
  - > Guides must prepare for their adventures one hour before the office opens, and they must stay one hour after closing to properly dry and store the equipment.
  - > Administrative assistant must have adventure bookings ready the day before.

The adventure guides are trained professionals who are able to do all adventure bookings and are qualified to instruct any of the training courses offered by Double N Adventures.

>Note to Student—Workweek Dates

There are many time-sensitive activities in this text. Your instructor will assign dates for both the workweek and the trade show. Since you will be required to find flights for the trade show and book appointments, it's necessary for the trade show date to be a real, future date so that accurate information can be found.

	Realtime date
Week of	Feb. 8 - 12
Monday's Date	Feb. 8
Trade Show* Date	Apr. 23, 24, 25

* Trade shows are held on Fridays, Saturdays, and Sundays and should be dated accordingly.

For example

	Realtime date
Week of	Monday, November 15, to Sunday, November 21, 2010
Monday's Date	November 15, 2010
Trade Show* Date	December 3, 4, & 5, 2010

Adventures

The company brochure (see next page) lists the services offered by Double N Adventures, including a brief description of each adventure, and the fees. (The same brochure is available under "Student Resources" at http://www.doublenadventures.nelson.com. You should print a double-sided copy of the brochure for quick reference.)

notes

Ideas for Businesses

Your staff members deserve the best. They deserve to be treated to a day of fun and adventure.

Consider booking a "corporate adventure" to reward your staff for their continued loyalty and support. After all, a business is only as good as its employees.

We offer a variety of corporate adventures that include everything necessary to create a memorable and electrifying experience.

There is no better way to improve teamwork and boost morale!

This could be you!

Double N Adventures

93 Red Cliff Road
Treasure Bay, NL   A9V 2K8

Put Label Here

DOUBLE N Adventures

This could be you!

AN EXPERIENCE TO REMEMBER

Tel: 1-877-807-4214

The Adventures are Endless...

At Double N Adventures, we believe that everything can be an adventure. We strive to make each experience offered a unique and exciting one.

However, our number-one priority is safety. You will be in the care of trained professionals at all times and before many of our adventures, you will be required to complete some safety training.

Our goal is to provide you with an adventure that will be stimulating and exhilarating.

This could be you!

Price List

Here is a list of our current adventures.
Prices are per person.

Canoeing (min. 4 people) $150.00
A 6-hour canoe trip into the wilderness. Includes all equipment, tour guide, and lunch.

Kayaking (min. 3 people) $200.00
A 4- to 5-hour kayaking trip in the Atlantic Ocean. Includes all equipment, tour guide, and lunch.

Rafting (min. 2, max. 7 people) $175.00
A 2-hour adventure that takes you into some rapids. Includes all equipment, tour guide, and return transportation from the river's end.

Caving (min. 3 people) $100.00
A 6-hour adventure, including a 2-hour hike to and from a remote cave, 1 hour of guided exploration, and lunch.

Fishing (min. 2 people) $225.00
A 4-hour adventure. Includes all equipment, lunch, and boat ride. Seasonal fishing. Call our office for dates available.

Rock Climbing (min. 2 people) $125.00
A 4-hour adventure. Includes training and all safety equipment.

Water-Skiing $175.00
A 3-hour adventure that includes lessons and all safety equipment.

Various Training Programs . . . . $$.$$
Safety training, Wilderness Survival training, First Aid training, etc. Please call for prices.

This could be you!

DOUBLE N Adventures

93 Red Cliff Road
Treasure Bay, NL   A9V 2K8

Phone Number:
(709) 807-4214

Toll-Free Number:
1-877-807-4214

adventures@DNA.com

Clip art used with permission from Microsoft.

Adventure Details

It is important to understand what each adventure involves. Table 1 provides a detailed list of each adventure offered by Double N Adventures, including the length, fee, minimum and maximum number of people per guide, and the equipment necessary.

*every guide needs a GPS/cell phone

> **tip**

For example, if a canoe adventure is planned for six people, you will need to book two guides, three canoes, eight life jackets, and one GPS and order eight lunches and ten waters (always supply two extra bottles of water).

TABLE 1 Detailed List of Double N Adventures						
Adventure	Length (in hours)	Fee (per person)	Minimum number of people	Maximum number of people per guide	Maximum number of people per adventure	Equipment	Comments
Canoeing	6	$150	4	5	15 clients; 3 guides	Canoes (3 people per canoe) Life jackets (1 per person) 1 GPS 1 Cellphone Bag lunch (1 per person) Water	Guide is not required in each canoe
Kayaking	4-5	$200	3	3	9 clients; 3 guides	Kayak (1 person per kayak) Life jackets (1 per person) 1 GPS 1 Cellphone Bag lunch (1 per person) Water	
Rafting	2	$175	2	7	21 clients; 3 guides	Raft (8 people per raft) Life jackets (1 per person) 1 GPS 1 Cellphone	

Company Policies and Procedures

TABLE 1 Detailed List of Double N Adventures (continued)

Adventure	Length (in hours)	Fee (per person)	Minimum number of people	Maximum number of people per guide	Maximum number of people per adventure	Equipment	Comments
Caving	6	$100	3	8	24 clients; 3 guides	Helmet with light (1 per person) 1 GPS 1 Cellphone Bag lunch (1 per person) Water	
Fishing	4	$225	2	4	8 clients; 2 guides	Pleasure craft Life jackets (1 per person) 1 GPS 1 Cellphone Bag lunch (1 per person) Water Fishing gear (max. 4 per boat) Tackle box	One speedboat/ pleasure craft; max. 8 clients per boat; when more than 4 clients, take turns fishing; lunch on a beach; ½- to 1-hour trip to and from
Rock Climbing	4	$125	2	3	9 clients; 3 guides	Safety harness (1 per person) 1 GPS 1 Cellphone	1 hour training prior to hike
Water-skiing	3	$175	3	3	3 clients; 1 guide	Pleasure craft Life jackets (1 per person) 1 GPS 1 Cellphone	Lessons given prior to skiing
First Aid/ Safety Training*	6	Varies		15		Bag lunch (1 per person) Water Training Booklets	Max. class size is 30

* Wilderness survival training, Wilderness first aid training, GPS navigation training, Map & compass training.

Equipment List

- 7 three-person canoes
- 14 one-person kayaks
- 1 pleasure craft—speedboat*
- 6 GPSs
- 6 cellphones
- 4 rafts
- 30 life jackets
- 30 helmets with lights
- 1 tackle box
- 6 fishing rods
- Printed training manuals
- Rock climbing equipment for 20 people

* Note: Water-skiing and fishing use the same boat

Source: Paulo Resende/Shutterstock

notes

Office Setup

You should set up your office as you would set up your real office. Being able to find what you need, when you need it, is a skill. Being organized in an office setting is an incredible time saver. Below are a few simple guidelines and tips to help you keep your office in tip-top shape.

- *Save files with a file name that is easy to find when you need it months later.* Developing a consistent file-naming system will save you time when you are looking for a document you need. Since the recipient's name is a very important element of letters, notices, memos, and the like, all invoices and client documents should be saved by *LastName FirstName* plus a description. For example, when saving a letter that has been sent out to a particular person, you should save that file as *LangMatthew_OverdueNotice (LastNameFirstName_OverdueNotice)* or *GrierBianca_TradeShowMay10 (LastName FirstName_SpecialEventInvitation)*. If the document is a general document that was sent out to a large number of clients, you can name it by using a description and the date—for example, *IntroducingNewTours_Nov10_2010*.

- *Keep everything professional.* E-mail is a common form of business communication; it is important to keep all internal and external messages professional. You should use proper punctuation, be brief and polite, and edit and proofread your messages. Do not use chat lingo, ALL CAPITALS (shouting), or all lowercase letters.

- *Set up a to-do list for your tasks.* You should keep a single list of everything you need to do. Record on your to-do list all of your tasks and submit this list to your instructor. Tasks that are to be completed on a different day should be recorded on all daily to-do lists until that item is finished and passed over to the person who requested it. For example, if Georgia asked you on Tuesday to generate a list of client names for her by Thursday, you should record that request on Tuesday's to-do list. If the task isn't completed on Tuesday, you should carry it over to Wednesday's to-do list, and so on. Once the list has been generated, record the task "pass completed list of client names to Georgia" on Thursday's to-do list. A to-do list accomplishes the following:

  > It keeps track—in one place—of all the tasks you need to complete.

  > It helps you prioritize your work by listing the most important jobs first, thereby ensuring you don't waste time on trivial tasks.

  > It reduces your stress and keeps you organized and focused on the most important tasks.

  > It makes you more reliable, since you won't forget any tasks.

- *Develop your telephone skills.* The way you answer the telephone will form the customer's first impression of the business. Always be polite, and identify yourself and the organization when answering the telephone—for example, say, "Good morning. Thank you for calling Double N Adventures. This is [your name]. Would you like an adventure today?"

- *Adding attachments.* For the purpose of this book only, when attaching a file to an e-mail, type "Attachment: *document name*," at the end of the e-mail—for example, *Attachment: brochure.docx*. This will demonstrate that you know a file needs to be attached to the e-mail. Your instructor may request that you send a real e-mail with an attachment to demonstrate that you can perform the task.

Adventure Booking Payments

Clients must secure their booking with a 50 percent down payment two weeks prior to the adventure. The balance is due the day before their adventure. (Because some adventures will start before you arrive at work, all bookings must be paid for a day in advance.)

Invoicing

You must create an invoice at the time of booking. Once an invoice has been paid in full, add a PAID watermark in red font, 80 percent lighter. The PAID watermark should be applied so that it is placed diagonally on the page.

Cancellations

The 50 percent deposit is fully refundable for cancellations received 48 hours or more before the scheduled adventure. Otherwise, the deposit is nonrefundable.

Bad Weather Guidelines

Occasionally, we must cancel an outdoor adventure because of unsafe weather. In such cases, clients can choose either to participate in an indoor training session on the originally scheduled day (offered first) or to reschedule their outdoor adventure.

Lunch Meetings

Lunch meetings include soup, sandwich, or wrap tray. In an effort to reduce waste and preserve our environment, we use our own cups for tea and coffee and our own glasses for water and drinks.

Source: Falk Kienas/Shutterstock

notes

Staff Requirements

All staff members must

- provide original school certificates and diplomas (Double N Adventures will keep photocopies of these on file);

- obtain an RCMP-certified criminal record check;

- show respect, understanding, and patience when guiding an adventure, and follow all staff adventure rules;

- arrive at work a few minutes early;

- wear appropriate attire and safety equipment at all times when guiding an adventure;

- ensure that clients wear safety equipment at all times during an adventure;

- ensure that clients sign the necessary waivers before starting their adventure;

- keep their first aid training and adventure guide training up to date; and

- maintain equipment, including performing routine inspections as mandated by Transport Canada, and report any equipment deficiencies on the appropriate form.

notes

Document Preparation

In an effort to keep all correspondence consistent, Double N Adventures follows specific formatting rules, outlined below.

1. Write all forms of documentation (letters, reports, memos, and so on) on company letterhead.
2. Use standard block style when writing letters.
3. Letters of two or more pages must have a second page header that includes the company name and phone number, as well as the page number. This header does not go on the first page.
4. In all letters, use open punctuation.
5. Use Times New Roman 12-point font for all documents.
6. When using Word 2007, remove extra spacing from the address and closing.
7. When adding new clients to the database (if in Excel), use red font so they can be easily identified.
8. Record each day's revenue on a *Daily Deposit Form*. Record refunds as a minus.
9. Update the *Equipment Booking List* daily.
10. Complete an *Adventure Guide Check Sheet* for each adventure on the day before the adventure.
11. Complete invoices as soon as an adventure is booked. A 50 percent deposit is required two weeks prior to the adventure, with the balance due 24 hours before the adventure.
12. Maintain a daily to-do list.
13. Record all adventures in the schedule upon booking.
14. Record all meetings and appointments in the appropriate staff members' schedules upon booking.
15. Fax *Brown Bag Lunch Forms* before 5 p.m. on the day prior to an adventure booking.
16. Use *While You Were Out* forms to record phone calls for staff members who are out of the office.
17. Complete *What Happened Today* forms daily.

> **tip**
>
> To remove automatic extra spacing from a section of text in a Word 2007 document, highlight the appropriate line(s), and then, from the Home tool bar in the Paragraph group, click on the Line Spacing button and choose "Remove Space After Paragraph."

Company Policies and Procedures

Source: Roxane Rowsell

Equipment Booking List

You must book the necessary equipment for each adventure by using the *Equipment Booking List* (see Figure 1). (The complete Excel spreadsheet is located under the "Student Resources" link on the book's companion site at http://www.doublenadventures.nelson. com.) The spreadsheet uses formulas, so when you enter the equipment needed for Adventure 1, the *Number Remaining* and *Total* columns will be automatically updated. You must save a new file for each workday.

Figure 1

Equipment Booking List

Item	Number	Number Remaining	Adventure 1	Adventure 2	Adventure 3	Adventure 4	Adventure 5	Total
Canoes	7	7						0
Kayaks	14	14						0
Speed Boat	1	1						0
Raft	4	4						0
Tackle Box	1	1						0
Fishing Rods	6	6						0
Life Jackets	30	30						0
GPSs	6	6						0
Cellphones	6	6						0
Helmets with Lights	30	30						0
Rock Climbing Harnesses	20	20						0

Schedules and Calendars

Scheduling is a very important part of the administrative assistant's job. You are responsible for keeping all schedules and calendars up to date. You have access to the following schedules:

- Nick Rockwell's schedule

- Noah Rockwell's schedule

- Georgia Taylor's schedule

- *Daily Adventure Schedule**

* You are the only person who has administration access to the *Daily Adventure Schedule* (see Figure 2). This means everyone can view the file, but only you can add, remove, or update it. (This Excel spreadsheet is located under the "Student Resources" link on the book's companion site at http://www.doublenadventures.nelson.com.)

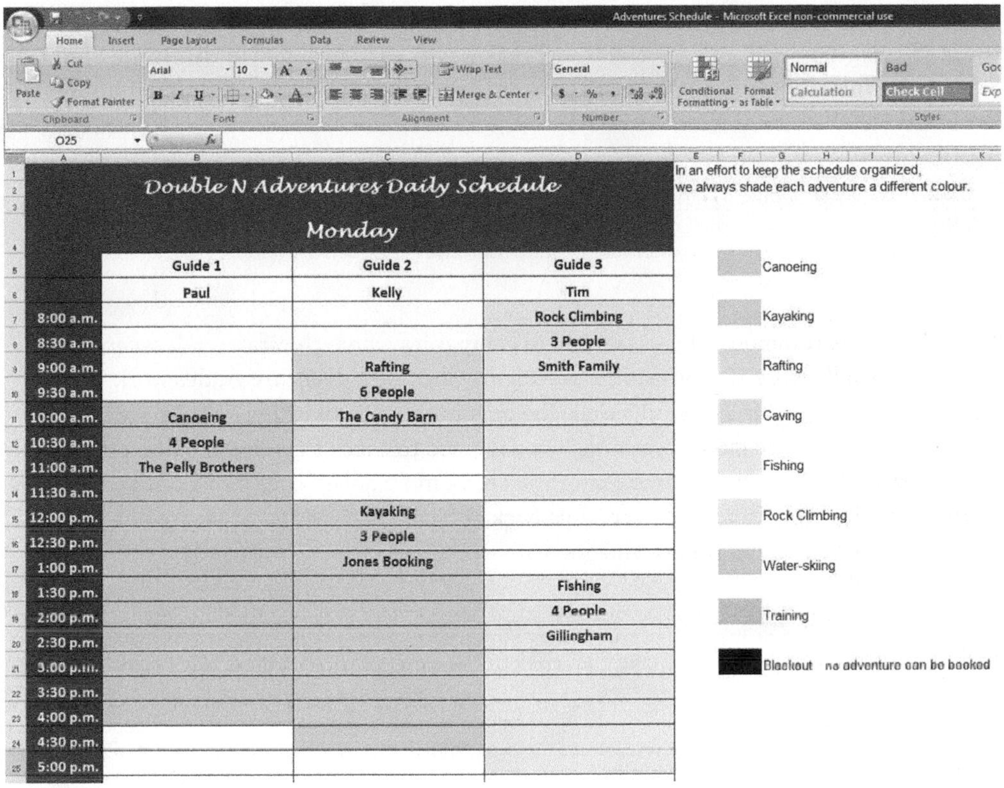

Figure 2
Daily Adventure Schedule

Double N Adventures Daily Schedule

Monday

Time	Guide 1 — Paul	Guide 2 — Kelly	Guide 3 — Tim
8:00 a.m.			Rock Climbing
8:30 a.m.			3 People
9:00 a.m.		Rafting	Smith Family
9:30 a.m.		6 People	
10:00 a.m.	Canoeing	The Candy Barn	
10:30 a.m.	4 People		
11:00 a.m.	The Pelly Brothers		
11:30 a.m.			
12:00 p.m.		Kayaking	
12:30 p.m.		3 People	
1:00 p.m.		Jones Booking	
1:30 p.m.			Fishing
2:00 p.m.			4 People
2:30 p.m.			Gillingham
3:00 p.m.			
3:30 p.m.			
4:00 p.m.			
4:30 p.m.			
5:00 p.m.			

In an effort to keep the schedule organized, we always shade each adventure a different colour.

- Canoeing
- Kayaking
- Rafting
- Caving
- Fishing
- Rock Climbing
- Water-skiing
- Training
- Blackout   no adventure can be booked

Staff Schedules

The schedules for everyone who works in the office, as well as the boardroom schedule, are set up in an Excel file (see Figure 3). This file should be viewed electronically because it is large and printing the schedule would waste paper. Schedules need to be updated regularly, and keeping an accurate schedule is extremely important. The schedule, which shows all the changes made throughout the week, will be submitted only on Friday. Figure 3 shows what the schedules file looks like.

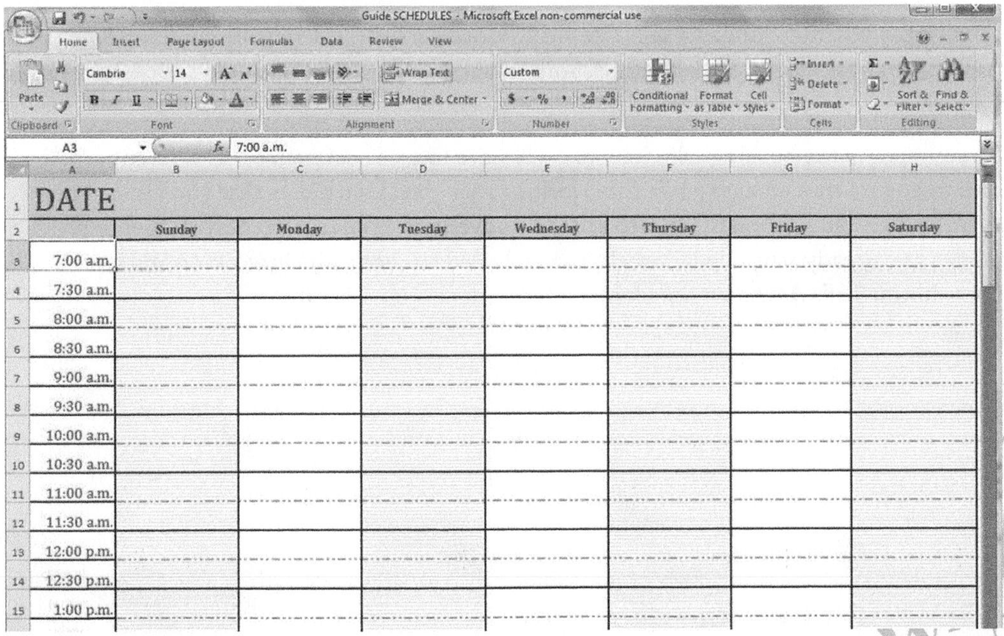

Figure 3
Schedules

DATE

	Sunday	Monday	Tuesday	Wednesday	Thursday	Friday	Saturday
7:00 a.m.							
7:30 a.m.							
8:00 a.m.							
8:30 a.m.							
9:00 a.m.							
9:30 a.m.							
10:00 a.m.							
10:30 a.m.							
11:00 a.m.							
11:30 a.m.							
12:00 p.m.							
12:30 p.m.							
1:00 p.m.							

Double N Adventures: A Complete Office Simulation

You will notice that this Excel file contains separate schedules for Nick, Noah, Georgia, and the staff (please see Figure 3a - Schedules Breakdown). Also included in this is the Staff Schedule, which is based on a three-off, two-on, two-off, three-on schedule, commonly known as the "3 and 2, 2 and 3" schedule.

Figure 3a
Schedules: Breakdown

◄ ◄ ► ►I **Nick's Schedule** / Noah's Schedule / Georgia's Schedule / Boardroom / Staff Schedule / ☜
Ready

This schedule is common in hospitals and in companies where the staff work seven days a week and usually work 12-hour shifts (see Figure 3b). The adventure guides work 11-hour shifts, but this schedule still works well. The only problem is that there are days when you don't have enough guides working. You will need to check the schedule daily and on a regular basis throughout your workday. If you have more adventures booked than you have guides available, you should first schedule Nick or Noah. If Nick and Noah are not available, you can call in one of the guides who are off.

Figure 3b
Schedules: Monthly

	A	B	C	D	E	F	G	H	I	J	K	L	M	N
1		Month 1												
2		Mon	Tue	Wed	Thu	Fri	Sat	Sun	Mon	Tue	Wed	Thu	Fri	Sat
3	Paul's Schedule				Paul	Paul			Paul	Paul	Paul			
4	Rebecca's Schedule	Rebecca				Rebecca	Rebecca			Rebecca	Rebecca	Rebecca		
5	Kelly's Schedule	Kelly	Kelly				Kelly	Kelly			Kelly	Kelly	Kelly	
6	Tim's Schedule	Tim	Tim	Tim				Tim	Tim			Tim	Tim	Tim
7	Nick's Schedule (as needed)													
8	Noah's Schedule (as needed)													
9														
10														
11		Month 2												
12		Wed	Thu	Fri	Sat	Sun	Mon	Tue	Wed	Thu	Fri	Sat	Sun	Mon
13	Paul's Schedule				Paul	Paul			Paul	Paul	Paul			
14	Rebecca's Schedule	Rebecca				Rebecca	Rebecca			Rebecca	Rebecca	Rebecca		
15	Kelly's Schedule	Kelly	Kelly				Kelly	Kelly			Kelly	Kelly	Kelly	
16	Tim's Schedule	Tim	Tim	Tim				Tim	Tim			Tim	Tim	Tim
17	Nick's Schedule (as needed)													
18	Noah's Schedule (as needed)													
19														

Finally, the schedule file has a separate sheet for the boardroom in your building. Everyone has access to the boardroom schedule. Your job is to ensure that no double bookings happen.

As you update the booking schedule, you will have to cross-reference the different schedules to ensure that enough guides are working each day. Remember that you can call in extra guides, but you might need to schedule adventure bookings on days that enough guides are already scheduled to work. You will need to check who is working and assign them in the *Daily Adventure Schedule*.

Tips for Painless Calendar Management

Calendar management is the task that consumes the largest portion of admins' time (cited by 68 percent), according to a survey by the American Management Association (AMA). Fortunately, there are ways to make the job easier, more efficient, and less time consuming.

Avoid Communication Breakdown

Ask your boss about his or her preferences and priorities. Communication can make both your lives easier. You and your executive should agree on the following:

- What meetings your executive should attend and how you make that judgment.

- What time of the day is best for meetings. What are your supervisor's preferences? You may not be able to accommodate all of his wishes, but you can try.

- When and how you will go over your manager's schedule. Some admins and their bosses prefer a weekly meeting on a Monday or Friday to go over the next week's meetings. Others prefer daily, short meetings. The idea is to establish a regular time to review scheduling as well as a method for making changes and keeping the executive informed.

- What schedule format your boss prefers. Some managers love technology and will want their schedules put on handhelds, such as a Palm Pilot or a BlackBerry. Others prefer a paper system. Some managers fall between the two extremes—maybe they'll want a hardcopy, but they'll also want it on their desktop computer and their laptop.

  Judy Root has served as secretary for several presidents at the Interlochen Center for the Arts, a nonprofit educational institution in Michigan. Her last president, whom she served for five years, preferred a paper organizer. Her new boss wants his calendar online. She's currently learning the ins and outs of Microsoft Outlook for scheduling.

- Your boss's other preferences. Does your supervisor want to be interrupted during a meeting if it runs over? Can you determine which meetings you should schedule, or do you need to run everything by her? How much time does she need between meetings?

Educating the Boss

Communication is a two-way street. Besides finding out how your executive wants his schedule handled, spend time explaining how you would like to manage his schedule. Unless your supervisor objects, it will be easier for you to manage her calendar if you're the only one who can schedule appointments. Sometimes a supervisor will be shy about having you schedule personal appointments such as a doctor's appointment or an at-home cable TV installation. If your boss wants access to the calendar, spend time documenting how your role as gatekeeper will benefit both of you. If she insists on getting involved, develop a system so that you'll be in the loop about any changes she makes.

Company Policies and Procedures

Double N Adventures: A Complete Office Simulation

Scheduling Tips

Confirming all meetings 24 hours or 48 hours in advance can save you and your boss unwanted headaches. Your boss won't waste time prepping for a meeting that's been cancelled. It will also ensure that you catch any mistakes, such as scheduling conflicts.

Consider these other suggestions:

- **Judge a meeting by its organizer, and adapt the schedule accordingly.** If a meeting called by your company's vice president of sales routinely runs 30 to 45 minutes over its allotted time, block out that amount of time on your executive's calendar. In the same vein, if another executive is always extremely punctual, make sure your boss gets to the meeting on time.

- **Try to bundle meetings together and have them all in the morning or the afternoon to reduce interruptions.**

- **Keep one calendar** *only*. It's easier and more efficient to keep one calendar for your boss instead of distinguishing between personal and business appointments. Says Izsak: "[Keeping] two or three simultaneous calendars—one on the Palm Pilot, another on the computer, another in a Day Planner doesn't work. It gets too confusing." That doesn't mean your executive can't keep copies of the same calendar on different electronic devices—only that he shouldn't have more than one calendar. If your executive's calendar must be kept on the network and accessible to all, pre-emptively block out time. That will help funnel requests to you. It will also help your boss have enough time to get his job done in addition to attending meetings.

- **Be flexible.** If you're scheduling a meeting with your boss and 20 other executives, don't expect to get everyone in the same room, at the same time, on the same day. "You'll never get 20 people to agree on one time—it's hard enough with just four," says Jean Custato CPS/CAP, an administrative assistant for the legal department of a health care company in Massachusetts. Instead, prioritize. Who absolutely *needs* to be there? Pick the date and time when the most people who are most critical to the meeting can make it.

- **Pick your boss's priorities.**

- **Use software to the fullest.** Calendar programs such as Microsoft Outlook, Lotus Notes, and Office Accelerator have made admins' lives a lot easier. But such programs are only as good as the person using them. Be sure you know how the software works and how to use its advanced features. If you don't, request some training or buy a book or CD on the program.

- **Pad the time between meetings.** Colin Cairns, communication director at Christie Communications, a public relations, marketing, and advertising agency in Santa Barbara, California, always keeps one hour free for his boss each day. That way, she has time to handle unexpected emergencies. "If every minute is scheduled in advance, there is never time to deal with an immediate crisis," Cairns says.

- **Find "overlooked time" for meetings.** For example, use time that your boss would otherwise spend waiting in an airport.

- **Act like a diplomat.** Try to be positive rather than negative when scheduling appointments. Says Cairns: "If clients and employees feel important and know that you're trying your best to get a convenient and timely meeting scheduled, they will be more willing to work with you.".

- **When possible, combine meetings.** That is, schedule multiple meetings on the same topic. Obviously, this is more efficient.

No matter how well you plan a day, there will be changes, cancellations, and additions. But if you follow the tips presented here, you'll find that managing a calendar needn't be stressful and time consuming.

Source: "Counting the Days" by Jenny C. McCune from *OfficePro* Magazine, Jan/Feb 2004, published by International Association of Administrative Professionals.

Source: Roxane Rowsell

Establishing a Daily Routine

Before you start, here are a few things to keep in mind. What will you have to submit to your instructor at the end of each chapter? You will need to read each chapter in detail to find that out exactly.

Here are some suggestions to help keep you on track. Note that all the forms mentioned below are available as templates under the Student Resources link at http://www. doublenadventures.nelson.com.

To-Do List

- *Always* maintain a daily to-do list (see Figure 4) and submit it as one of your tasks.

- Your to-do list should include everything you had to do on that day and some items may carry over to the next day's list.

- Submit everything you are required to do for *that* day. If something is required for another day, submit it on the day it is required. Do not submit it on the day it was requested.

Figure 4
To-Do List

Daily To-Do List

_____
_____
_____
_____
_____
_____
_____
_____
_____

Message Pad

Record every telephone message by using the *While Your Were Out* form (see Figure 5).

Figure 5
While You Were Out

To	
Date	Time

While You Were Out

Name	
Of	
Phone	Ext.

Telephoned	☐	Please Call	☐
Stopped by the Office	☐	Urgent	☐
Wants to See You	☐	Will Call Back	☐

Message

Adventure Guide Check Sheet

You must fill out and submit a *Adventure Guide Check Sheet* for each booking (see Figure 6). This sheet provides your guides with all the required information about their adventures. These sheets must be completed the day before the scheduled adventure because the guides start work an hour before you do—they need time to get everything ready. Remember, there may be days when a guide has more than one adventure scheduled, so they will need more than one check sheet. You will need to complete these check sheets and hand them in to your instructor. They should be saved as guide's *lastnamefirstname_date_adventure*—for example, *ReeganTim_2010-08-22_rafting*

Figure 6
Adventure Guide Check Sheet

Adventure Guide Check Sheet

DATE _____

GUIDE'S NAME _____

ADVENTURE _____

TIME _____

Total Number (Including Guides) _____

Equipment List	#Needed

Manuals	# Needed

Lunches Ordered	#Needed

Company Policies and Procedures

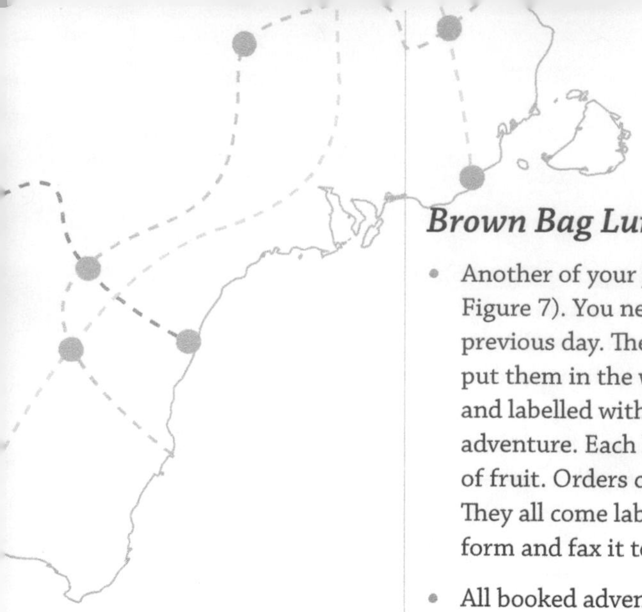

Brown Bag Lunch Form

- Another of your job responsibilities is ordering lunches for every adventure (see Figure 7). You need to have the order for tomorrow's lunches submitted early on the previous day. The local restaurant, Mac's Deli, will deliver your "brown bag lunches" and put them in the warehouse refrigerator (they have a key). The lunches arrive bagged and labelled with the guide's name so they only need to grab one bag labelled for their adventure. Each lunch includes a deli sub sandwich, two cookies or a muffin, and a piece of fruit. Orders contain a variety of sandwiches. You do not need to choose any types. They all come labelled, and each order will include at least one veggie sub. Complete the form and fax it to 709-639-4778.

- All booked adventures that include a lunch must have two extra bottles of water per adventure.

Figure 7
Brown Bag Lunch Form

BROWN BAG LUNCH FORM

Date: _____

GUIDE'S NAME _____

Total Number (Including Guides) _____

GUIDE'S NAME _____

Total Number (Including Guides) _____

GUIDE'S NAME _____

Total Number (Including Guides) _____

GUIDE'S NAME _____

Total Number (Including Guides) _____

notes

_____

_____

_____

_____

_____

_____

_____

_____

What Happened Today Form

- Because it is impossible for you to submit every part of this project to your instructor, a *What Happened Today* form must be submitted daily (see Figure 8). This form has two purposes:

  > First, it is a way for you to review your workday to ensure that everything is complete.

  > Second, it will provide your instructor with a quick overview of the work you have submitted.

- You will need to create your own summary of the jobs you have completed. You can consider this sheet a summary of your day.

What Happened Today

What Guides are working today?

What Appointments did you book?

Who did you send e-mails to?

How many Brown Bag lunches were ordered for tomorrow?

Who are the Guides working tomorrow?

How many Adventures are booked for tomorrow?

Guide	Adventure	Time

Did you add anyone to the database today?

What new Adventures did you book today?

Date	Customer	Adventure	Time

Other important information:

Figure 8
What Happened Today Form

Company Policies and Procedures

> **tip**

When reading through the chapters, develop a list of what will be expected of you. This list will help you understand what you need to submit to your instructor.

Additional Information

- You will be given a "Monday Checklist" to help you get into the groove and understand what is expected of you.

- On Tuesday, you will be given a "don't forget" list.

- You will not receive any lists on Wednesday, Thursday, and Friday to remind you what needs to be submitted.

Questions for Review

1. What is the name of the company?

   Double N Adventures

2. What is the nature of this company's work?

   provide daily adventures

3. Who are the supervisors?

   Nick Rockwell   Georgia Taylor
   Noah Rockwell

4. What information can be found in the tip boxes?

   How to complete day to day tasks.

5. What information is located on the associated website?

   templates

6. What are the office hours?

   8 AM - 5 PM

7. What are the hours for the adventure guides?

   7 AM - 6 PM

8. How many employees does the company have?

   eight

9. List the employees and their titles.

Nick Rockwell - Owner
Noah Rockwell - Owner
Georgia Taylor - Office Manager
Megan Benoit - Admin. Assistant
Paul - Guides
Recbecca - Guides
Kelly - Adventure Guide
Tim - Guide

10. What is the company slogan?

Want to go on a
Would you like

11. What is the required format for namin

Names are typed in

Source: Wolfgang Amri/Shutterstock

Source: dpullicino/iStockphoto

Monday

What you will practise today

> Prepare various administrative documents, such as meeting agendas, minutes, deposit slips, and lunch orders.

> Manage operations, including the schedule for the boardroom and various meetings.

> Accurately transcribe voice mail messages.

> Maintain the schedules for the office managers and adventure guides by using Microsoft Excel.

> Manage Information requests and prospective client data.

> Promote the company when creating materials, such as reports and fax cover sheets.

> Maintain and track client data, and respond to the requests of prospective clients.

> Demonstrate professionalism and creativity when generating marketing materials.

You are the administrative assistant for Double N Adventures. In that role, you will be making decisions about what will be completed today and what you need to submit. You will have to think about the information given to you in this book's Introduction and decide what needs to be done. You've been informed of the office's daily events, the forms you'll need to fill out daily, the organization involved, and so on. Refer back to the Company Policies and Procedures section often to make sure you're following the company's requests. Remember that every company does things slightly differently.

notes

> tip

As discussed in the Introduction, make sure you order tomorrow's brown bag lunches and complete tomorrow's *Adventure Guide Check Sheet*. Also, don't forget to check the *Equipment Booking List*.

Nick and Noah are the owners of Double N Adventures. They have worked hard to build a large client base and dream of the day when their company will be known all over Canada. You are their administrative assistant, and today you are going to have a very busy day.

It is part of your job to maintain an electronic calendar for Nick, Noah, and Georgia. These three calendars must be up to date at all times. You are expected to add appointments, change meetings, and remove entries. You receive few specific instructions for this task. Remember that you are no longer a student. Your employers expect you to use the skills you have learned. They also expect you to show initiative in completing each part of your job with maximum professionalism.

notes

8:00 A.M.

It's Monday morning, and you're eager to start work. One of the great things about your job is that you're always busy. This helps the day go faster. It also means you have to be highly efficient if you're going to complete all your work.

The first thing you do every day is make sure all of today's adventure bookings are ready. You turn on your computer to check your e-mail and voice messages. Before you can get started, you hear the front door open.

Source: KennStilger47/Shutterstock

> tip

Make a *Memo Template,* using the sample provided as your guide.

- Save this as *Memo Template* to use in the future.
- Remember to place the company's logo on the memo.
- Begin to draft this memo for Georgia. Note that you don't have all the information you need.

8:05 A.M.

Georgia has just arrived at the office. She tells you there will be a staff meeting next week. The purpose of the meeting will be to discuss each employee's role at an upcoming trade show. She asks you to write a memo telling all employees that their attendance is required. The meeting will last at least two hours. You will get more information for this memo later. For now, make sure your memo includes all the necessary details. If any guides cannot attend because they are scheduled for an adventure, you will need to provide them with a copy of the meeting's minutes. Georgia also needs you to prepare the minutes from the last meeting. She will give them to you tomorrow.

You are required to create a memo that includes the company's logo. An electronic copy of the logo can be found under the "Student Resources" link on this book's companion website (http://www.doublenadventures.nelson.com). You are also required to create a memo template. A template is simply an empty file with the heading in place. You will be opening it to create all future memos, and when you save this file, it will create a new .docx file for you, leaving your template file (.dotx) intact for the next time you need it. By using template files (.dotx), you ensure that your template remains a blank document. Be sure to follow the rules for spacing and formatting memos.

Source: Stan Cook/Stan Cook Sea Kayaking Adventures

Once you have the information you need to schedule this meeting, and the memo is completed, forward it to the staff via e-mail. (For the purposes of this book, your e-mails will be message files that you save, not actual e-mails.)

Besides all of this, you will need to book the boardroom for a meeting. You will find the boardroom calendar under "Student Resources" on this book's website.

Do you need to do anything else to prepare for this meeting? Should you order coffee?

> tip

When you book a meeting, you need to record it on the calendars of those who must know about it. So for this meeting, you will need to record it on following calendars:

- Nick
- Noah
- Georgia
- Boardroom
- *Adventure Schedule* (apply blackout)

8:35 A.M.

You have finished discussing the memo with Georgia. Now you can go back to checking your messages. You have two new e-mails and two voice messages.

The first e-mail is from Nick and is time-stamped 8:30 a.m. (see Figure 1.1).

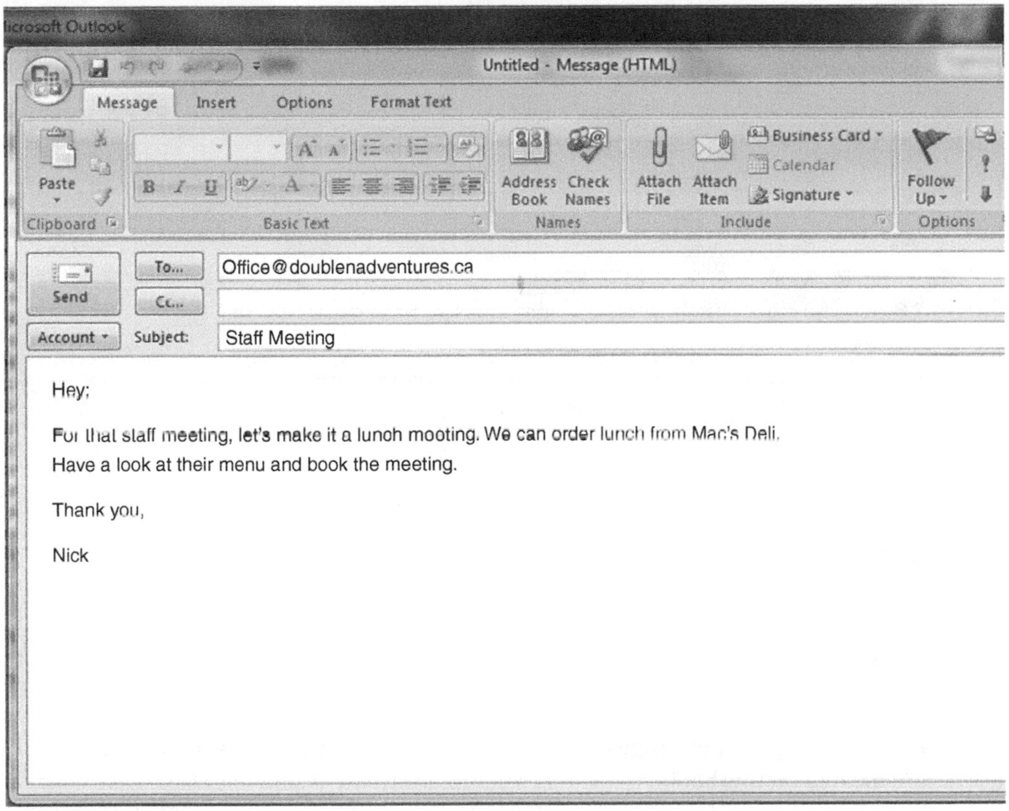
Untitled - Message (HTML)
Message
Insert
Options
Format Text
Paste
Clipboard
Basic Text
Address Book
Check Names
Names
Attach File
Attach Item
Business Card
Calendar
Signature
Include
Follow Up
Options
Send
To...
Cc...
Account
Subject:
Office@doublenadventures.ca
Staff Meeting
Hey;
For that staff meeting, let's make it a lunch mooting. We can order lunch from Mac's Deli.
Have a look at their menu and book the meeting.
Thank you,
Nick

Figure 1.1
Outlook Message: Nick

notes

• The second e-mail is from Noah and arrived at 9:15 a.m. (see Figure 1.2)

Figure 1.2
Outlook Message: Noah

> **tip**

Always look at the time of your e-mails and messages. You should check them in the order they arrived.

> **tip**

When tour guides are rescheduled, you need to record the changes in the Excel schedule file. For reasons of both payroll and liability, it is important to keep track of scheduling changes.

Microsoft Outlook — Untitled - Message (HTML)

Message | Insert | Options | Format Text

To... Office@doubleadventures.ca
Cc...
Subject: Payment?

Hi there;

Did we ever receive the down payment from Mr. Pico for the booking he made a few weeks ago? He was planning on treating his staff to a rafting adventure. He wanted to build team spirit and increase morale.

If he hasn't made the down payment yet, could you please send him a letter letting him know that it's past due and in order to maintain his booking, it must be paid net/10 days.

His information is in the database.

The down payment required is 50%.

Let me know if he paid.

Thanks,

Noah

You notice your telephone message light flashing. To listen to your voice mail, open the audio files located on this book's website in a subfolder titled "Audio Files." Each workday is represented by a separate folder on the website. In this book's pages, audio file icons in the margins alert you that you need an audio file from the website to complete your task.

• The first message received is from Nick and was recorded at 6 a.m.

• The second message received is from Rebecca and was recorded at 7:32 a.m.

Go to
http://
www.doubleadventures.
nelson.com to listen to Nick's
message.

Go to
http://
www.doubleadventures.
nelson.com
to listen to Rebecca's
message.

38

9:30–10:00 A.M.

You've now checked all your messages, have jotted down a to-do list, and have begun to work on these tasks. You usually take your coffee break from 10:00 a.m. to 10:15 a.m. but you are very flexible about this—much depends on what's happening at that time. Since no one is in the office, you decide to take a quick coffee break.

10:15 A.M.

You arrive back at your desk and check your e-mails and voice messages. There are no new e-mails, but you do have one new voice message.

* There is a new phone message from Georgia. It was recorded at 10:05 a.m.

10:30 A.M.

Nick, Noah, and Georgia have discussed their need for a database and have created an outline of what they want in an Excel file. Now they want you to open this file and use the information to create a Microsoft Access Database or an enhanced Excel spreadsheet. Your instructor will provide you with further instructions. Once you have created this, your employers want you to record all contact information in it. You can start working on it today, but you have until Wednesday to finish it. You spend the rest of the morning working on your assigned tasks.

Roger Flemming arrives to pay the balance on his rock climbing adventure, which is booked for Wednesday. He pays with cash.

12:00–1:00 P.M.

The office is closed for lunch.

Go to
http://
www.doublenadventures.
nelson.com
to listen to Georgia's
message.

> tip

Prepare a list of at least five different items that can be used as promotional materials. Prices, pictures, and the website should be included on your list.

> tip

When preparing your report, don't forget to include a cover page, a contents page, page headers, and an appendix. The form Noah is completing will be attached as Appendix A.

1:00 P.M.

You return to the office after lunch and notice that Noah is rushing around. He's going to need something done in a hurry! He goes to his office and after a few minutes appears in front of you with a bunch of handwritten notes. "Please," he says, "compile these into a report by the end of the day." He has just learned that Double N may qualify for a Hire a Student grant, but the application deadline is 9 a.m. tomorrow. He will complete all the necessary forms and paperwork, but he needs you to prepare some additional information and present it to him as a two- to three-page informal report.

He has given you some basic information (see Figure 1.3):

Figure 1.3

Hire a Student Grant Report Information

Who we are ...

You can complete this section for me.

What we do ...

I need you to write up a couple of paragraphs about the company.

What a student would do ...

A student would be responsible for assisting our adventure guides with equipment, supplies, and training. The student would have to prepare the equipment and properly clean and store the equipment after each outdoor adventure. This would be a wonderful learning experience for any student.

Desired Student Background

Our local college teaches a two-year Adventure Tourism program. We would be interested in offering one of the first-year students a summer position. (Add something about their skills, etc.)

Our Contribution

Ideally, we would be looking for a 100% funded student; however, we would consider a 20% contribution toward wages. Add more information about being a small company, still building clientele, etc.

Write a paragraph thanking them for considering us.

Provide our contact information for follow up. This report should be at least two pages, but no more than three. I'll review it after you have completed it.

Thanks.

Noah

40

Double N Adventures: A Complete Office Simulation

1:30 P.M.

Georgia is back from her meeting with Tammy Kellows and has asked to see the promotional material you have found. She wants to review it and decide which one she will order. You have the list ready, so you e-mail it to her. Make sure to include the link to the website where you found this information.

3:00 P.M.

While you were busy at the photocopier, you received a phone message from Tammy Kellows. She is very interested in booking an outdoor adventure as a reward for her top 10 sales staff. First, though, she wants to see the company's brochure and price list.

Check all adventures that are booked for tomorrow. Complete the following: *Adventure Guide Check Sheet*, *Equipment Booking List*, and *Brown Bag Lunch Form*.

Amy Sheppard has just called to book a kayaking adventure for four people on Thursday of this week. She would like the booking from 8:30 a.m. to 1:30 p.m. She wants to pay the entire amount now, using her Visa card. Her contact information is: 2439 Penwell Blvd., Grand Falls-Windsor, NL A3T 1V9. Telephone (709) 479-2121.

Go to
http:// www.doublenadventures. nelson.com
to listen to Tammy's message.

> **tip**

Any time you obtain contact information for a customer or client—or anyone you may need to get in touch with again—make sure to add that person's information to your database.

Source: Roxane Rowsell

3:30 P.M.

Two of your responsibilities are (1) to accept booking payments, and (2) to check invoices to see who has paid in full and who has not. Full payment for adventure bookings is due the day before the adventure. You need to check the invoices to see who still has to pay the balance on their account. All payments received should be recorded on a *Daily Deposit Form.*

Source: Roxane Rowsell

Before you leave the office at the end of the workday, make sure everything is ready for the next day's adventure bookings. Have the lunches been ordered? Are the forms ready? Are enough guides scheduled? Is all the equipment booked? Are all of tomorrow's adventure bookings paid in full?

Use the *Submission Check Sheet* on the next page to ensure that you've completed all your tasks. Also, fill out the *What Happened Today* form.

notes

Submission Check Sheet

Below is a list of all the tasks you should have completed for Monday. Use this *Submission Check Sheet* to ensure that you have every task completed and ready to submit to your instructor.

JOBS/TASKS	Completed	Comments
Create *Memo Template*		
Write memo for staff meeting		
Book staff meeting in all schedules, including the Adventure Schedule		
Send e-mail to staff and attach memo		
Create invitation		
Check Mr. Pico's invoice, act accordingly, and send a follow-up e-mail to Noah		
Set staff meeting		
Record Rebecca's sick day and add Paul to the schedule		
Find promotional material		
Record Georgia's meeting with Tammy Kellows at 1 p.m.		
Write report for Noah		
Add Tammy Kellows to the database		
E-mail Tammy Kellows with the information requested		
Check next day's bookings and complete the *Adventure Guide's Check Sheet*, *Equipment List*, and *Brown Bag Lunch Form*		
Complete the *What Happened Today* Form		
Complete the *Daily Deposit Form*		
Make a to-do list (always)		
Complete booking for Amy Sheppard		

Discussion Topic

All in a Day's Work

You get a call from an angry customer who tells you she had booked an adventure for her husband as a surprise for his 45th birthday only to discover that he heard your voice on their answering machine confirming details. The surprise is ruined because you left a message for her that her husband overheard. What do you do?

_____

_____

_____

_____

Code of Ethics for Administrative Professionals

Members of the International Association of Administrative Professionals® (IAAP) have established four standards of professional conduct for administrative professionals. The IAAP defines these professionals as "individuals who are responsible for administrative tasks and coordination of information in support of an office related environment and who are dedicated to furthering their personal and professional growth in their chosen profession."

Ethical behaviour is encouraged by both the Code and the profession. Each administrative professional has a personal obligation to support and follow the Code of Ethics. Those who violate the code risk losing the respect of professional colleagues and the trust of employers, clients, and society and could be penalized by the association or profession.

1. The administrative professional shall act as a trusted agent in professional relations, implementing responsibilities in the most competent manner and exercising knowledge and skill to promote the interests of the immediate and corporate employer.

2. The administrative professional shall strive to maintain and enhance the dignity, status, competence, and standards of the profession and its practitioners.

3. The administrative professional shall insist that judgments concerning continued employment, compensation, and promotion be based upon professional knowledge, ability, experience, and performance.

4. The administrative professional must consider the promotion and preservation of the safety and welfare of the public to be the paramount duty.

Source: International Association of Administrative Professionals, http://www.iaap-hq.org.

Source: Stan Cook/Stan Cook Sea Kayaking Adventures

Tuesday

What you will practise today

> Manage information requests from prospective clients via e-mail.

> Prepare minutes from handwritten notes.

> Analyze data, and use that information to generate tables and to produce both bar and pie charts.

> Prepare administrative documents, such as supplies order forms.

> Complete jobs by using office software, such as Microsoft Word, Excel, and Access (Access will be optional as determined by your instructor).

> Create and maintain a client database.

> Maintain equipment and adventure booking schedules.

> Manage and process customer payments and prepare the necessary documentation.

> Create an agenda by using templates available at http://www.microsoft.com.

In this chapter, you will have the chance to demonstrate a wide variety of office skills. You will complete jobs that require you to use Microsoft Excel, Microsoft Word, and e-mail.

notes

Yesterday was a busy day. Today will also be busy, since three adventures are booked. It is beautiful outside, so the outings will go ahead as scheduled. You must check tomorrow's schedule to ensure that the equipment is booked, the lunches are ordered, and the correct number of guides are scheduled. Once all of your guides are off on their adventures, it's time for you to begin your daily tasks.

You should have a morning list of things to do to make sure the adventures run smoothly.

9:00 A.M.

First you check your e-mail and telephone messages. You have received an e-mail from the Web master. It is your responsibility to answer or redirect any Web inquiries generated from your website. Today's e-mail is a simple request for more information (see Figure 2.1).

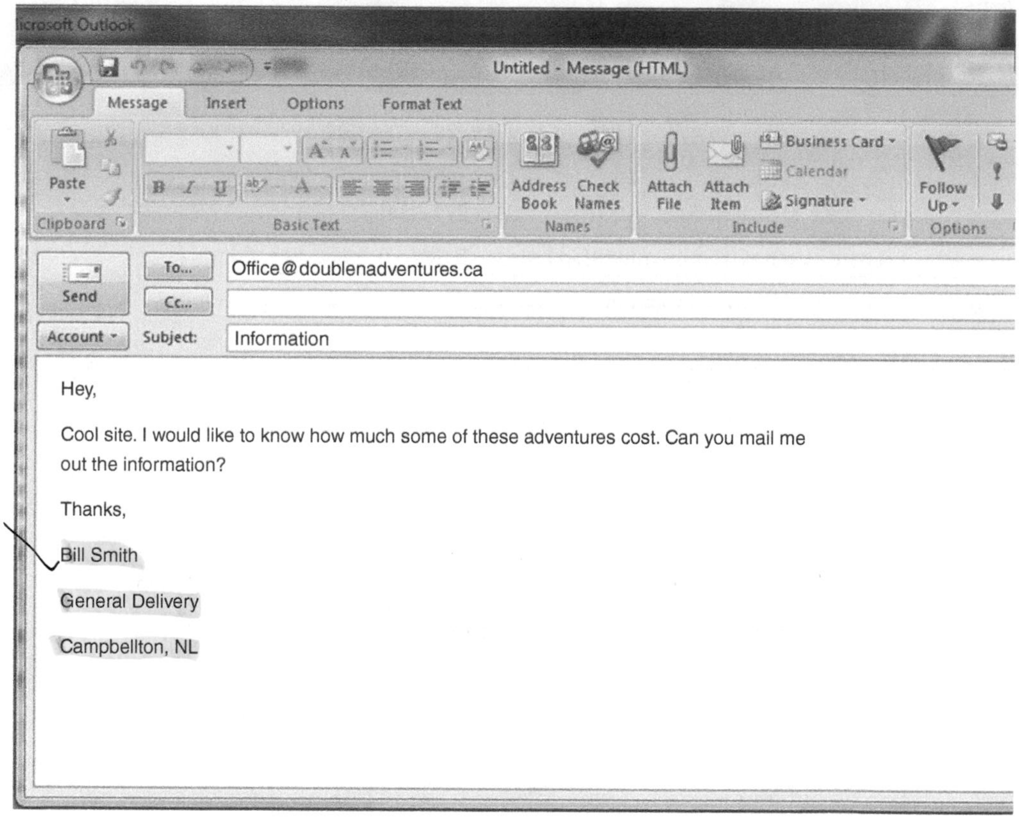

Figure 2.1
Outlook Message: Bill Smith

> **tip**

If you need a postal code, you can look it up on the Canada Post website at http://www.canadapost.ca.

Write a short email thanking Bill Smith for his interest in the company and telling him you've attached a company brochure that lists the adventures offered, along with pricing information. Make sure you add him to the contacts database. Did you notice that he forgot to include his postal code? Bill's e-mail address is bill.smith@nf.sympatico.ca.

Georgia hands you the notes from the last staff meeting and asks you to have them ready for her by Friday (see Figure 2.2).

Figure 2.2
Minutes from Staff Meeting

Double N Adventures
Board Room

Date – two weeks ago [replace with a real-time date based on the date of your work week]

9:00 a.m. to 10:00 a.m.

Minutes

Participants

Nick, Noah, Georgia, [your name]

Welcome

The meeting began at 9:00 a.m. with Nick chairing. Nick welcomed everyone to the teleconference.

Minutes

The minutes of the [date one month prior to the above date] meeting were reviewed and approved as circulated.

Equipment—Nick discussed the need for patches to be available for emergency use in personal flotation devices (PFDs). There was a lot of discussion regarding ordering new PFDs versus repairing older ones. We need to do some research or at least post the current research on safety issues.

Food Allergies—Georgia mentioned she'd heard a friend saying she would like to have an adventure complete with bagged lunch, but worried her egg allergy may prevent her. What can we do about this type of situation? We can have the option to order "special" lunches. How do we get the word out that we can accommodate people with food allergies?

Trade Show—Noah suggested that we book two tables at the upcoming trade show. We need to know the cost first. Kelly will research the costs for us.

Prizes/Giveaways—Georgia suggested items that would appeal to outdoor adventure types. She will compile the information about how much we can spend and how many prizes.

Continued

Department of Tourism Funding—Nick is in the process of trying to secure funds from the Department of Tourism for promotional items. He has a meeting next month with one of Tourism's staff and will advise if any information becomes available.

Supplies—Georgia mentioned that the coffee, tea, etc., have been replenished with all the gifts that came in over the holidays. She asked that all staff members clearly identify their own mugs by writing their names on the bottom by using a waterproof marker.

Meeting Adjourned at 9:45 a.m.

Action Items

Nick to forward guidelines to [your name] to review safety issues regarding the PFDs

Georgia to research what alternative lunches can be provided for those with food allergies

[Your name] to research giveaways after Georgia sends the dollar amount

Source: Roxane Rowsell

9:30 A.M.

You notice that you're getting low on several office supplies. Send an e-mail to Nick, Noah, and Georgia asking them if they need any supplies. Let them know the order will be placed on Thursday. Start your list now. Create a table for supplies needed. Make sure you include item names, item numbers, and the prices. Supplies are ordered from Staples, and all the information for ordering can be obtained from http://www.staples.ca. You already know you will need to order the following:

- 2 Black toner for HP Colour LaserJet 1600
- 2 boxes of name tags
- 100 name tag badges
- 4 packages of card stock paper
- 6 boxes of pens (red, blue and black)
- 10 small note pads
- 6 boxes of staples

You receive an incoming telephone call from Billy Thompson of U Save Insurance. He asks to speak with Nick. Have Nick call him at (709) 807-4973.

10:00 A.M.

You receive an e-mail from Tammy Kellows. After meeting with Georgia, she has decided to book a rafting adventure for 10 to 12 of her staff. Tammy wants to book it for two weeks from Friday and would prefer an afternoon booking.

Georgia gave you Tammy's business card (see Figure 2.3).

Figure 2.3
Business Card: Tammy Kellows

10:30 A.M.

Nick walks into the office grinning from ear to ear. His meeting at the Department of Tourism went well. He needs you to work some magic with his past three years' statistics. "I need this to look snazzy. You know I'm not great with Excel, so could you please create a very professional-looking table and a couple of different charts? And I really need this by the end of the day."

Nick has maintained a very plain table in Excel showing the increase in the number of different adventures booked over the past three years (see Figure 2.4). You can find this file on the book's website under the "Student Resources" link. The file is located in the *Tuesday* folder and is called Stats_for_DoubleNAdventures.xlsx.

> tip

When creating a table or chart for a government department, make sure your logo is on each page.

Figure 2.4
Adventure Booking Statistics

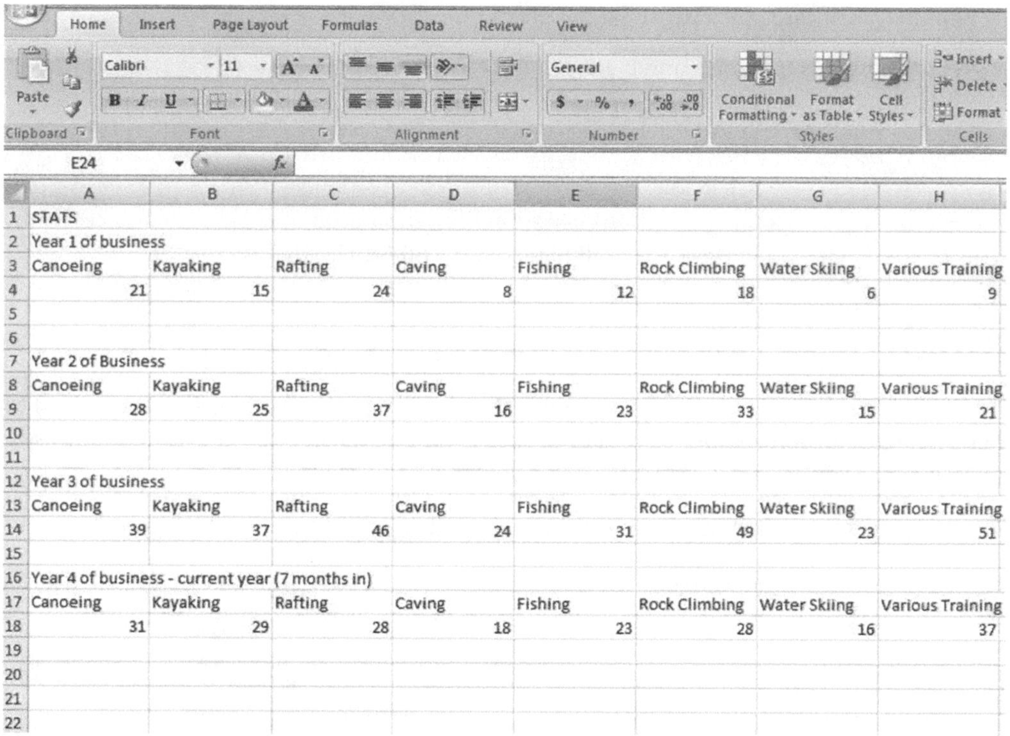

	A	B	C	D	E	F	G	H
1	STATS							
2	Year 1 of business							
3	Canoeing	Kayaking	Rafting	Caving	Fishing	Rock Climbing	Water Skiing	Various Training
4	21	15	24	8	12	18	6	9
5								
6								
7	Year 2 of Business							
8	Canoeing	Kayaking	Rafting	Caving	Fishing	Rock Climbing	Water Skiing	Various Training
9	28	25	37	16	23	33	15	21
10								
11								
12	Year 3 of business							
13	Canoeing	Kayaking	Rafting	Caving	Fishing	Rock Climbing	Water Skiing	Various Training
14	39	37	46	24	31	49	23	51
15								
16	Year 4 of business - current year (7 months in)							
17	Canoeing	Kayaking	Rafting	Caving	Fishing	Rock Climbing	Water Skiing	Various Training
18	31	29	28	18	23	28	16	37
19								
20								
21								
22								

He doesn't care what the colours are as long as they look professional. He doesn't want the result to be too bright or crazy. Each year should be clearly visible and should clearly indicate the increase in the number of adventures booked over the previous years (see the sample bar chart in Figure 2.5).

Make a workbook with the table on Spreadsheet #1, the previous years as a column chart on Spreadsheet #2, and this year's pie chart on Spreadsheet #3. Make sure you name the spreadsheets, include the company logo on each, and provide all necessary information. Remember that you will be submitting this to the Department of Tourism, so it needs to be perfect.

The end result of this task should look much like what you see in Figure 2.5. You must include each adventure and each year. Keep in mind that each chart must include a title centred at the top and that the x and y axis need to be labelled appropriately. And don't forget the legend! The colours are not important, as long as they look professional.

When creating a workbook with more than one page, make sure you rename the pages and keep your colours and fonts consistent.

> tip

When making the column chart, you will need to graph all three years. Creating a new table would be wise. Don't forget to use the Help feature if you need to.

Figure 2.5
Sample Bar Chart

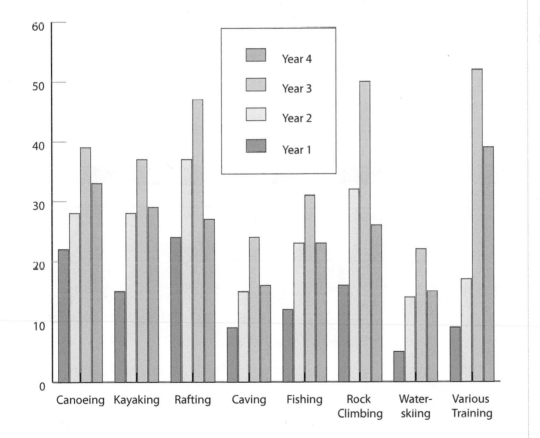

Use the same statistics to make a pie chart showing this year's breakdown of adventure bookings. Use the 3D chart with the names and percentages (%), as illustrated in the sample pie chart in Figure 2.6.

Figure 2.6
Sample Pie Chart

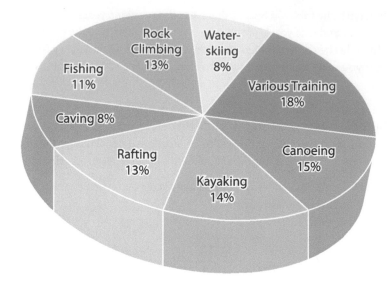

Remember to use a chart title and a legend when necessary.

Ronald Jeffery just stopped by the office to pay the remainder of the balance on his adventure. He paid with cheque #43.

1:00 P.M.

The staff meeting is planned for Monday of next week from 11 a.m. to 1 p.m. Lunch will be provided at the meeting. Compile a list of things you need to do to prepare for the meeting. Order the lunch and make sure you have coffee and tea in the office. E-mail all staff to ask whether anyone has anything to include on the agenda. Let the staff know they must let you know by the end of Thursday whether they have anything to include.

Create an agenda template. Use the "meeting agenda" or "agenda" template found in the templates on your computer or located online. Now start the agenda. You already have the following information:

- Town meeting update—Noah

- New bookings—Georgia

- Department of Tourism—Nick

- Trade show update—Nick

- Promotional material—You

Remember that this agenda can be saved today and finished later in the week once you get all the information. It will not be submitted with today's work.

From time to time, you are asked to send letters—to the mayor, to your local Member of Parliament (MP), and so on. Go onto the Internet to find the name, address, and telephone number for your mayor, your local MP, and the minister for your province's Tourism Department.

Source: Ron Hilton/Shutterstock

> **tip**

You now know the time of the staff meeting. Make sure you book it in everyone's schedule and order lunch.

53

Chapter 2 Tuesday

> **tip**

To access the templates, click on the Office button, then New, then Find Agendas. If the agenda you're looking for isn't there, type "agenda" in the Search bar at the top to search Microsoft Office Online.

2:30 P.M.

Nick has asked you to do some research for him. He needs you to write a letter to the provincial tourism minister. The letter will ask the minister to look at Double N's promotional materials and website and to include Double N in the provincial *Travel Guide*.

Nick also wants you to add the minister's contact information to the company database. When doing so, include the name and contact information of the minister's secretary. Use your provincial government's website to find this information.

Michael Lenning stopped by the office to book a rock climbing adventure for three people on Friday. He pays the entire amount with cheque #378.

His information is PO Box 91, Gander, NL, A1V 2R7. Phone (709) 671-0003.

4:00 P.M.

You've just received an e-mail from Noah asking you to do some Internet research (see Figure 2.7). Double N has decided to investigate magazine advertising. He and Nick want you to research magazine circulation numbers.

> **tip**

When addressing the minister of any government department, refer to that person as The Honourable.

> **tip**

When creating a table, arrange it in a logical manner. For example, you could list elements alphabetically, chronologically, or in ascending or descending order. Consider the importance of each table element. In this case, the magazine circulation numbers are most important. Remember this when deciding how to arrange and present the table.

Figure 2.7
Outlook Message:
Advertising

Microsoft Outlook — Untitled - Message (HTML)

To... Office@doublenadventures.ca
Subject: Advertising info

Hi,
We are considering doing some advertising in some of the most popular magazines. Can you get me the circulation numbers for the following magazines? Last year's figures are fine.

People	Family Circle
Oprah's Magazine	Car and Driver
Martha Stewart's Magazine	Sports Illustrated
Reader's Digest	Women's Health
Men's Health	Endless Vacation
Rachel Ray's Magazine	National Geographic
Good Housekeeping	Better Homes and Gardens

Put the information into a table for me and have it ready by tomorrow morning. I want to have time to review this before our staff meeting.

Thanks,
Noah

Don't forget to complete your daily tasks.

JOBS/TASKS	Completed	Comments
Check next day's bookings and complete the *Adventure Guide's Check Sheet*, *Equipment Booking List*, and *Brown Bag Lunch Form*		
Complete the *What Happened Today* form		
Complete the *Daily Deposit Form*		
Always make a to-do list		

Discussion Topic

All in a Day's Work

You have a problem. One of the most prominent business people in your area is a wonderful employer and loves to take his employees on elaborate retreats every year. He has been spending a lot of time in your office. This person has the potential to be a very big client. To date, though, he hasn't booked any adventures even though he's consuming a lot of your time. What should you do?

_____

_____

_____

_____

How to Be a More Productive Employee

The company you work for is paying you to do your job, so you must do it well. That said, you should also become a productive employee for the sake of your own personal growth. Being a productive individual provides greater satisfaction and boosts one's self-esteem. So improve your performance by making yourself more self-sufficient.

Follow these easy steps to becoming a more productive employee:

- **Being organized is the first step.** Organize your daily tasks by listing them. That way, you can properly keep track of your progress and avoid overlooking something. Keeping a task list is very helpful in all aspects of work, be it a simple chore at home or a big event for the company.

- **Prioritize the tasks on your list.** The harder tasks should be at the top of the list, the easier ones at the bottom.

- **Never try to do several different tasks all at once.** Doing so would defeat the purpose of your task list. Also, doing more than one task at a time can overwhelm you. So finish one task before doing the next. For a sense of accomplishment, cross a task off your list when you have finished it. You will start feeling proud of yourself.

- **Learn the difference between a distraction and a breather.** A distraction is anything that keeps you from working on the task at hand. A breather is a short break that lets you reset your mind and relax your muscles. Breathers can help fuel your desire to finish the work. An unnecessary phone call, for instance, is a breather, if you take about five minutes to chat with a workmate. The call is a distraction when it takes you an hour to get off the phone.

- **Get rid of other distractions in your work area.** For example, a cluttered desk can make you lose your focus. If you need to disconnect yourself from people for a while, simply close your door or turn off your cellphone.

- **Handle tasks with flexibility.** Even when you are highly organized at work, some things may go wrong that are beyond your control. Be ready to adjust.

- **Set deadlines for yourself.** Deadlines motivate you to finish a task.

- **When the next workday comes, do your list all over again, adding whatever new tasks have been assigned to you on the day.**

These simple steps will help you become a productive employee and strengthen your work ethic.

Source: Staff Contributor/HowToDoThings.com

Source: Pavel Cheiko/Shutterstock

Double N Adventures: A Complete Office Simulation

Chapter 3

Source: Maridav/ShutterStock

Wednesday

What you will practise today

> Create, design, and edit various materials, such as brochures, letterheads, business cards, and magazine advertisements, to promote the company.

> Prepare advertising materials by using desktop publishing and templates.

> Manage financial and accounting documents and complete necessary paperwork.

As an employee for a small business, you can expect to be handling a vast number of different tasks. This chapter focuses on desktop publishing as well as regular, day-to-day operations.

notes

8:00 A.M.

As usual, you arrive to work just before 8 a.m. and get started on your routine tasks, such as these:

- Making sure the adventure bookings are ready to go
- Getting the adventure bookings ready for tomorrow
- Checking your to-do list to see jobs that are due today
- Checking your e-mail
- Checking your voice mail
- Checking the schedules
- Checking the equipment
- Ordering lunches if necessary

Source: Roxane Rowsell

9:00 A.M.

A long e-mail has arrived from Noah (see Figure 3.1). It has been sent to the whole team. Read it carefully. The office is buzzing with excitement.

Figure 3.1
Outlook Message: Noah

Microsoft Outlook

Untitled - Message (HTML)

Message | Insert | Options | Format Text

Paste | Clipboard | B I U | A | Basic Text | Address Book | Check Names | Names | Attach File | Attach Item | Business Card | Calendar | Signature | Include | Follow Up | Options

Send

To... Allstaff@doublenadventures.ca

Cc...

Account ▾ | Subject: Big News

Hi everyone,

Yahoo! We did it! I just heard from the Department of Tourism and guess what? We've been awarded a $25,000 grant for promotional development.

As you know, we are just about to enter into our busiest season, so I want this to take top priority.

Thankfully, we have a talented administrative assistant (an assistant who can expect to hear more details shortly).

Thanks, everyone. We're doing fantastically!

Noah

Double N Adventures: A Complete Office Simulation

10:00 A.M.

Noah arrives at your desk and is very excited. He says, "This has to be your top priority today. Can you get me the first drafts of the new promotional material by the end of the day?" Noah really wants to see the brochure, business cards, and letterhead today, but he can wait until tomorrow to see the flyer/magazine ad.

Let's take a few minutes to review Noah's wish list for the promotional materials. He shows you a couple of brochures that he really loves. He wants the company's brochure to contain photos and to be very colourful. The information in the brochure you're designing will be the same as in the current company brochure. He gives you free rein to create and arrange it any way you like.

Figures 3.2 and 3.3 contain two sample brochures. Noah really likes the look of these, but neither is the perfect brochure for the company.

See the table below for a list of Noah's likes and dislikes of the two sample brochures. If you want, you can download and use a template as your starting point.

Likes	Dislikes
Review of Sample Brochure #1	
Inside layout	Front cover
Lines and graphic layout	It is not set up to double as a mailout like the brochure you have now, with a place for a mailing label.
Review of Sample Brochure #2	
Graphic lines that carry all the way across the brochure.	Colours
Different shapes for the pictures	It is not set up to double as a mailout.

notes

Figure 3.2
Sample Brochure #1

Comprehensive Financial Consulting Services

- Asset Accumulation
- Estate Planning
- Asset Allocation
- Education Planning
- Income Taxes
- Disability

FINANCIAL
Consultation

3561 Clarence Avenue North
Saskatoon, SK
S7H 2E3
(800) 555-0132
(306) 555-0133 fax
http://www.financialconsulting.ca

FINANCIAL
Consultation

FINANCIAL OBJECTIVES

INVESTMENT SOLUTIONS

Diversify **Your** Investments

The best way to protect yourself from the ups and downs of the market is to diversify your investments. We'll show you how to smooth out market risks to achieve positive performance in your portfolio. Learn how diversification will benefit you!

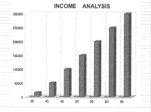

Addressing **Your** Financial Concerns

Financial concerns are one of the leading causes of stress in Canadian. We'll help you alleviate that stress with our expert financial planners. There are many options available to you, and our money experts will help put your money concerns behind you. We can help you with any or all of the following:

- estate planning
- education planning
- tax planning
- credit and debt management
- insurance planning

Our experts will ensure that all of your needs are addressed so that you can rest easy.

Securing **Your** Future

For more than 25 years, our company has been dedicated to retirement plan management. You're guaranteed to receive the best advice from approachable experts who are committed to securing your future.

Realizing **Your** Dream

You can have the financial freedom that you've always dreamed about. Our experts will control the risks you take, help you to achieve the independence and balance you want, and attain an even higher standard of living for you and your family. You won't be disappointed.

Figure 3.3
Sample Brochure #2

Using this information, you are now expected to create a brochure for Double N Adventures. Be creative, be original, and use consistent fonts and colours in all your promotional materials.

Next, review several business cards that Noah likes. He prefers the faded or ghosted image in the background (see Figure 3.4), and he thinks that a rafting image would be really impressive. Noah also likes the look of business cards that have a vertical or portrait orientation (see Figure 3.5).

Figure 3.4

Sample Business Card: Faded Background Image

Photo source:

Worytko Pawel/Shutterstock

FOURTH•COFFEE

Jane Doe
[President and CEO]

Phone: (780) 555-0101
Fax: (780) 555-0111
[4567 Main St., Edmonton, AB T5R 6A2]

[www.fourthcoffee.com]

Figure 3.5

Sample Business Card: Vertical or Portrait Orientation

Photo source:

Tyler Olson/Shutterstock

Your Logo Here

Your Name
Your Title

Organization Name
Primary Business Address
Your Address Line 2
Your Address Line 3
Your Address Line 4

Phone: (555) 555-555
Fax: (555) 555-555
E-mail: someone@example.com

Double N Adventures: A Complete Office Simulation

notes

There are many attractive business cards, and he wants you to create two different ones. The team will then select their favourite design.

Next, Noah wants you to create a unique letterhead. It is very important that you keep all the colours and fonts consistent. You're looking for a similar theme for the business. The Department of Tourism grant has given you the opportunity to give all your promotional materials a fresh and unique look. The image on each document must be the same, and the colour choices should be consistent.

notes

For the letterhead, Noah has more specific ideas. He wants it to have a strip of colour down the left margin and another strip of colour across the bottom. For the bottom, he wants the colour to fade out; then, to the far right, the colour will be light enough to have a place to put the contact information. Although it will be harder, he wants these strips or bands of colour to have a wavy look. Then he wants the logo at the top to the right. This letterhead will take some creative work and will involve some advanced desktop publishing skills. Noah does not want you to use a template for the letterhead. He wants this to be totally original. Double N Adventures must have a letterhead that is one of a kind.

He has drafted an image of what he would like the new letterhead to look like (see Figure 3.6).

Figure 3.6
Sample Letterhead

> **tip**

To create the waves on the letterhead, you can insert a shape, choose the curve, and draw a shape that looks like waves. The trick to making the waves look like they go all the way down the left side and continue across the bottom is to use two shapes. Have the shapes connect to look like one shape. Then you can apply different fill options to change the colour and to get the look you desire.

Double N Adventures: A Complete Office Simulation

1:00 P.M.

You receive a call from Jack Pelley. He wants to surprise his family with a caving adventure. He would like to book for his son, daughter-in-law, and three grandchildren who are coming home on Saturday, as well as for his daughter and her family. His son lives on the prairies and is coming home to Newfoundland for a couple of weeks. Jack would love to take them caving. The adventure should be booked for six adults and four children.

Book the caving adventure for next Thursday. Advise Mr. Pelley that a deposit will be needed to hold his spot. Create an invoice. Mr. Pelley will be in later today to pay for the full amount of the booking.

You have received a new booking message for Charlie Walsh (see Figure 3.7).

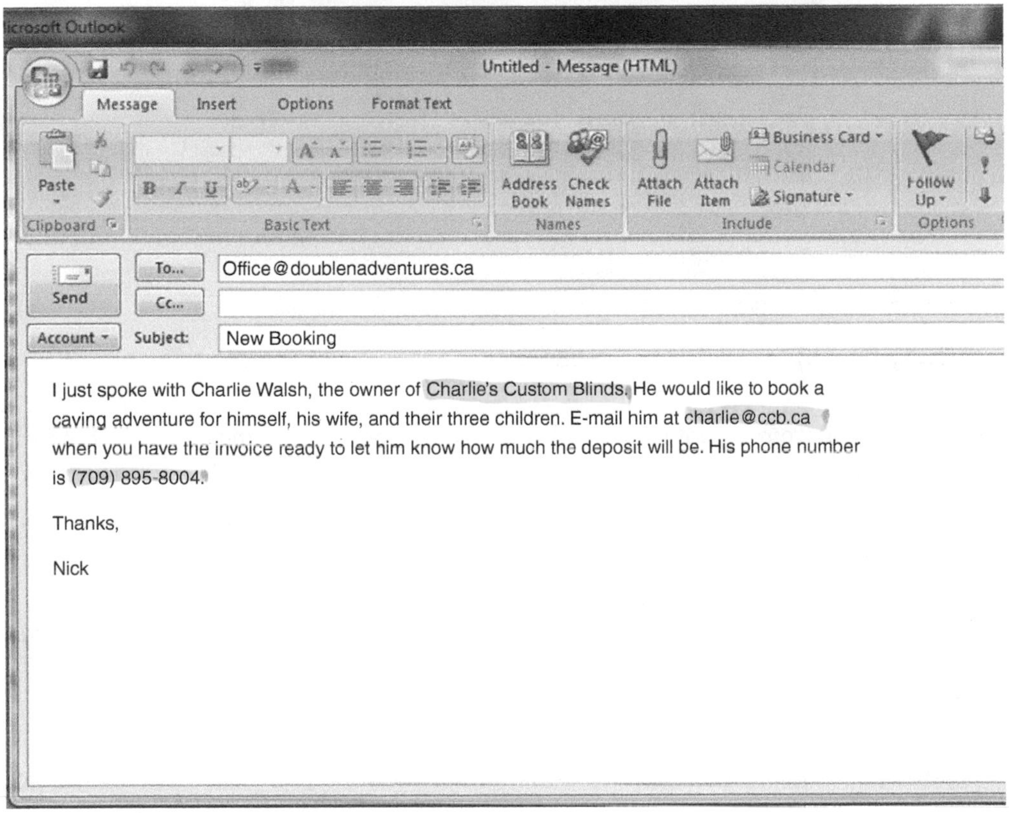

Figure 3.7
Outlook Message: New Booking

I just spoke with Charlie Walsh, the owner of Charlie's Custom Blinds. He would like to book a caving adventure for himself, his wife, and their three children. E-mail him at charlie@ccb.ca when you have the invoice ready to let him know how much the deposit will be. His phone number is (709) 895-8004.

Thanks,

Nick

After you call Charlie, you determine that the best date would be next Wednesday. You can e-mail him the rest of the information.

2:30 P.M.

Jack Pelley arrives to pay for the full amount of his booking. He pays by using his Visa card.

You spend the rest of the day completing your work.

Source: Roxane Rowsell

Discussion Topic

All in a Day's Work

You receive a call from a client who complains about the brown bag lunch. He does not feel this was enough food for that rigorous an outing. The customer is quite upset and wants a partial refund. How do you resolve this situation?

_____

_____

_____

_____

10 Tips For Creating Successful Business Presentations

Business is all about selling, whether it's a product, a topic, or a concept. When making a business presentation, the most important thing is to **know your material**. If you don't know everything about what you're selling, it isn't likely that the audience will buy it.

Keep your audience focused and interested. Making effective business presentations takes practise, but with a few tips up your sleeve, you'll be ready to take on the challenge.

Note—The following business presentation tips refer to PowerPoint (any version) *slides*, but all of these tips can be applied to any presentation.

1. Use Key Phrases About Your Topic.

Seasoned presenters use key phrases and include only essential information. Choose only the top three or four points about your topic and make them consistently throughout the *delivery*. Simplify and limit the number of words on each screen. Try not to use more than three *bullets* per slide. The surrounding space will make it easier to read.

2. Slide Layout Is Important.

Make your slides easy to follow. Put the title at the top of the slide where your audience expects to find it. Phrases should read left to right and top to bottom. Keep important information near the top of the slide. Often the bottom portions of slides cannot be seen from the back rows because heads are in the way.

3. Limit Punctuation and Avoid "All Caps".

Punctuation can needlessly clutter the slide. The use of all capital letters makes statements more difficult to read and is like SHOUTING at your audience.

4. Avoid Fancy Fonts.

Choose a font that is simple and easy to read, such as Arial or Verdana. Avoid script-type fonts as they are hard to read on screen. Use, at most, two different fonts—perhaps one for headings and another for content. Keep all fonts large enough (at least 24 pt but preferably 30 pt) so that people at the back of the room will be able to read without strain what is on the screen.

5. Use Contrasting Colours for Text and Background.

- Dark text on a light background is best, but avoid white backgrounds—tone it down by using beige or another light colour that is easy on the eyes. Dark backgrounds are effective for showing off company colours or if you just want to dazzle the crowd. In that case, be sure to make the text a light colour for easy reading.

- Patterned or textured backgrounds can reduce readability.

- Keep your colour scheme consistent throughout your presentation.

6. Use Slide Designs Effectively.

When using a *design theme* (PowerPoint 2007) or *design template* (earlier versions of PowerPoint), choose one that is appropriate for the audience. A clean, straightforward layout is best if you are presenting to business clientele. If your presentation is aimed at young children, select a layout that is full of colour and that contains a variety of shapes.

7. Limit the Number of Slides.

Keep the number of slides to a minimum. This will ensure that the presentation doesn't become too long and drawn out. It will also avoid the problem of having to constantly change slides during the presentation, which can be a distraction for your audience. One slide every minute or so minute is about right.

8. Use Photos, Charts, and Graphs.

Combining photos, charts, and graphs—and even embedding digitized videos with text—will add variety and keep your audience interested in the presentation. Avoid text-only slides.

9. Avoid Excessive Use of Slide Transitions and Animations.

While *transitions* and *animations* can heighten your audience's interest in the presentation, too much of a good thing can distract them from what you're saying. Remember, the *slide show* is meant to be a visual aid, not the focus of the presentation. Keep animations consistent in the presentation by using *animation schemes*, and apply the same transition throughout the presentation.

10. Make Sure Your Presentation Can Run on Any Computer.

Use PowerPoint's *Package for CD* (PowerPoint 2007 and 2003) or *Pack and Go* (PowerPoint 2000 and before) feature when burning your presentation onto a CD. In addition to your presentation, a copy of Microsoft's *PowerPoint Viewer* is added to the CD to run PowerPoint presentations on computers that don't have PowerPoint installed.

Source: © 2010 Wendy Russell (http://presentationsoft.about.com). Used with permission of About Inc., which can be found online at http://www.about.com. All rights reserved.

Source: Roxane Rowsell

Source: :Stan Cook/Stan Cook Sea Kayaking Adventures

Thursday

What you will practise today

> Understand travel-related terminology and time zone differences to finalize trip packages.

> Utilize research skills to determine best available flights.

> Apply decision-making skills to arrange and book hotels and car rentals.

> Prepare a detailed travel itinerary based on information gathered.

> Review and complete a purchase order.

> Use desktop publishing skills to create a PowerPoint presentation and business flyer.

Your role as an administrative assistant is evolving daily. This profession is not for someone who only wants to transcribe letters or take dictation. It's an exciting and challenging career—one that will keep you on your toes. Enjoy your day!

notes

9:00 A.M.

Adventures of Canada is a large trade show held once a year in Toronto. There is a long waiting list to attend this event. Today it's been confirmed that Double N Adventures is going to the trade show, which will take place next month (see Figure 4.1). You're required to make all the arrangements for the trade show today. Because you're one of the last exhibitors to secure a space, you need to make those arrangements fast. The flights and hotels could be hard to get.

The trade show will be held over three days from ___*April 23, 24, 25*___ _____ [*dates to be provided by your instructor*].

Figure 4.1

Outlook Message from Nick: Trade Show

Microsoft Outlook

Untitled - Message (HTML)

| Message | Insert | Options | Format Text |

Paste — Clipboard

B I U — A — Basic Text

Address Book — Check Names — Names

Attach File — Attach Item — Signature — Business Card — Calendar — Include

Follow Up — Options

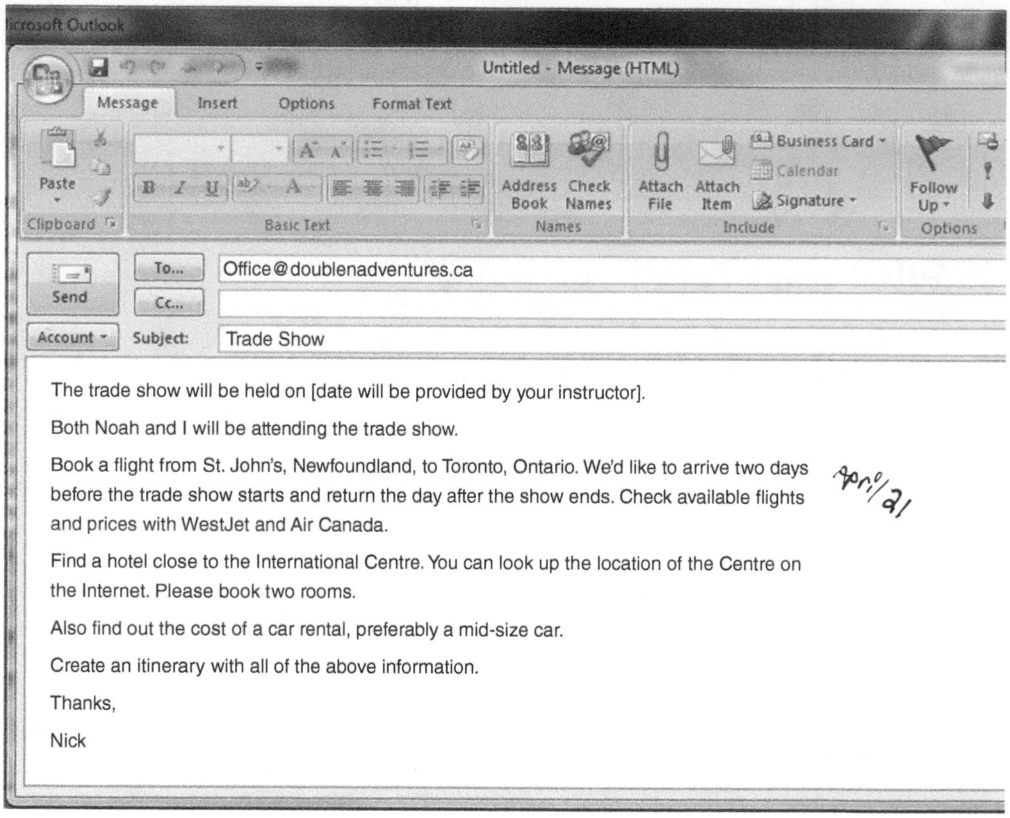

To... Office@doublenadventures.ca

Cc...

Account ▾ **Subject:** Trade Show

The trade show will be held on [date will be provided by your instructor].

Both Noah and I will be attending the trade show.

Book a flight from St. John's, Newfoundland, to Toronto, Ontario. We'd like to arrive two days before the trade show starts and return the day after the show ends. Check available flights and prices with WestJet and Air Canada. *April/21*

Find a hotel close to the International Centre. You can look up the location of the Centre on the Internet. Please book two rooms.

Also find out the cost of a car rental, preferably a mid-size car.

Create an itinerary with all of the above information.

Thanks,

Nick

Double N Adventures: A Complete Office Simulation

11:15 A.M.

Figure 4.2
Outlook Message from Georgia: Supplies Order

Microsoft Outlook

Untitled - Message (HTML)

Message | Insert | Options | Format Text

Paste | Clipboard | B I U | Basic Text | Address Book | Check Names | Names | Attach File | Attach Item | Business Card | Calendar | Signature | Include | Follow Up | Options

To... | Office@doubleadventures.ca
Cc...
Send
Account ▾ | Subject: | Supplies

I need you to order some black and red pens, Post-it notes, and a new stapler. And I also need three white D-ring, 1-1/2-inch binders with the clear front so we can insert a picture or something in the front.

Please order 100 page protectors as I'm planning to set up a binder of photos for the guys to take the trade show with them.

That's it for me!

Thanks,

Georgia

Go to
**http://www.
doubleadventures.
nelson.com**
to listen to William Taylor's message.

12:00 P.M.

Figure 4.3
Outlook Message from Noah: Trade Show Requests

Microsoft Outlook

Untitled - Message (HTML)

Message | Insert | Options | Format Text

Paste | Clipboard | B I U | Basic Text | Address Book | Check Names | Names | Attach File | Attach Item | Business Card | Calendar | Signature | Include | Follow Up | Options

To... | Office@doubleadventures.ca
Cc...
Send
Account ▾ | Subject: | Trade Show Requests

Hi,
We're setting up a computer at our trade show booth and would like a large monitor for easy viewing.
We need a PowerPoint presentation set up and here's what we need:
Use approximately 20 slides.
Use a lot of photos in the presentation (you can get these from our photo database).
Set it up as a show so that it runs automatically. It has to be set up to loop (play over and over).
The timing should be set at 15 seconds per slide.
Use some animation on the photos and random animation for the slide transitions.
There should be a maximum of 20 words per slide.
Always have the photo appear before the words.
Make sure you use the company logo and make it consistent with our new marketing material.
I think that's it for the presentation. Can you get this done for me today?
Thanks,
Noah

1:45 P.M.

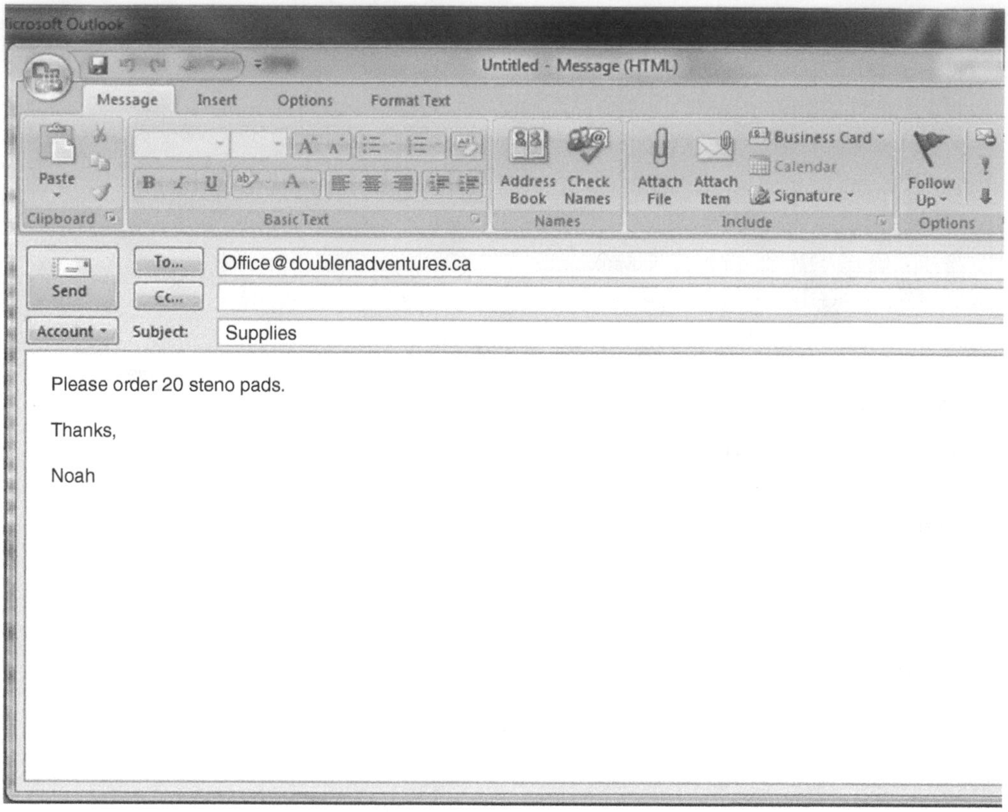

Figure 4.4
Outlook Message from
Noah: Supplies Order

Microsoft Outlook

Untitled - Message (HTML)

Message | Insert | Options | Format Text

To... Office@doublenadventures.ca
Cc...
Subject: Supplies

Please order 20 steno pads.

Thanks,

Noah

2:05 P.M.

Nick, Noah, and Georgia discussed the importance of having a flyer at their booth for the trade show. They want you to create one similar to the one in Figure 4.5. The flyer should include

- the company name;

- a list of adventures that Double N Adventures offers;

- the company logo; *and*

- contact information.

The flyer you create will also be used for a magazine advertisement and for local advertising. One feature that Noah likes is the half-faded look shown in the golf ad.

notes

Double N Adventures: A Complete Office Simulation

ATTENTION

7th Annual Golfapalooza

After a busy fire season, we are pleased to invite you to the end-of-season golf tournament.

Where: Gander Golf Club.
Drinks and barbecue at the Golf Club.

When: September 24th,
first tee time 12:30 p.m.

**Golf will be 18 holes,
foursomes, best ball.**

*Please sign below before
September 22nd
if you will be attending.*

Figure 4.5
Sample Flyer
Photo source:
Sylvaine Thomas/Shutterstock

> **tip**
>
> The image in the golf poster is the same picture twice. You insert two images, crop them so that they fit together to look like one image, then wash out or fade one image. You can use this tip to apply different kinds of faded looks. For example, you can create a faded centre.

73

Chapter 4 Thursday

notes

Figure 4.6
Outlook Message from
Noah: Supplies Order

Microsoft Outlook

Untitled - Message (HTML)

| Message | Insert | Options | Format Text |

Paste
Clipboard

B *I* U

Basic Text

Address Check
Book Names

Names

Attach Attach
File Item

Business Card ▾
Calendar
Signature ▾

Include

Follow
Up ▾

Options

To... Office@doublenadventures.ca

Cc...

Send

Account ▾   Subject: Supplies

I don't need any supplies this time.

Thanks,

Noah

Loretta King has just called to book a caving adventure for four people next Thursday. She will pay the deposit now and the balance next Wednesday. Loretta's contact information is 855 Battle Road, Halifax, NS B4T 0J0. Her phone number is (902) 547-8531. She pays the deposit by MasterCard.

Source: Stan Cook/Stan Cook Sea Kayaking Adventures

Figure 4.7
Outlook Message from
Georgia: Agenda

Microsoft Outlook

Untitled - Message (HTML)

| Message | Insert | Options | Format Text |

Paste — Clipboard — B I U — A — Basic Text — Address Book — Check Names — Names — Attach File — Attach Item — Business Card — Calendar — Signature — Include — Follow Up — Options

To... Office@doubleadventures.ca

Cc...

Account ▾ Subject: Agenda

Please add the Student Grant as New Business for the agenda.

Thanks,

Georgia

> tip

Remember to complete the required forms for tomorrow's adventure bookings.

3:30 P.M.

You receive a phone call from Michael Boyd, chairman of the Adventures of Canada trade show. He wants set up a conference call with Nick and Noah to discuss trade show procedures. This call is routine for first-time exhibitors. You schedule the call for Monday at 1 p.m. Eastern Standard Time. Michael Boyd's phone number is (416) 907-6689. He has assigned Double N Adventures Booth #117 for the trade show. The trade show will take place at the International Centre on Friday and Saturday from 10 a.m. to 10 p.m. and on Sunday from 10 a.m. to 6 p.m.

Source: Roxane Rowsell

4:10 P.M.

Figure 4.8
Outlook Message from
Noah: Agenda

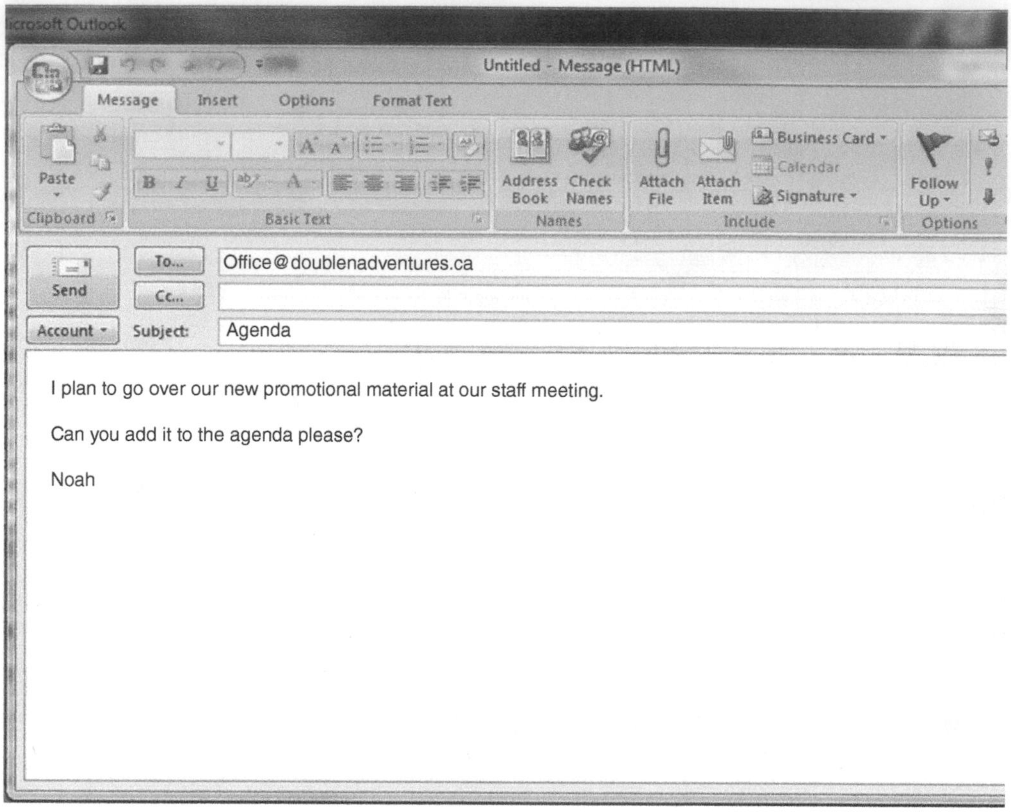

The trade show will be held in a different province. For that reason, you need to be aware of Canada's time zones and book appointments accordingly. You can find those time zones on the Internet. Or you can use Figure 4.9 - Canadian Time Zones map.

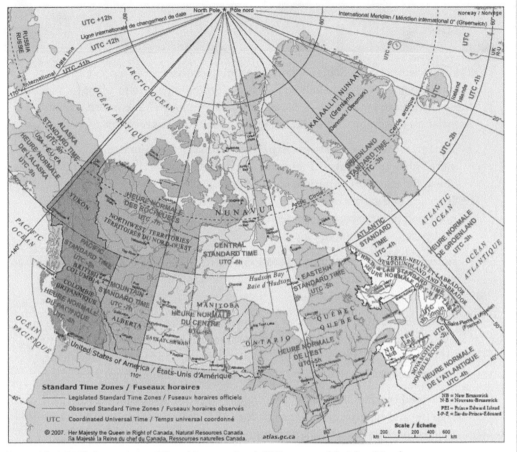

Source: Adapted with the permission of Natural Resources Canada 2010, courtesy of the Atlas of Canada.

Figure 4.9
Canadian Time Zones

Go to
http://
www.doublenadventures.
nelson.com
to listen to Ben Young's
message.

Discussion Topic
All in a Day's Work

You are alone at work and one of Nick and Noah's cousins show up. She wants to borrow one of the company kayaks for the weekend. You know that in the past, they have sometimes loaned out equipment, but they do not like to make a habit of it. You can't reach Nick or Noah to confirm this would be okay. What do you do?

Tips On Staying Ahead in a Changing Workplace

The office workplace is changing rapidly. Administrative professionals are being given greater responsibilities. What can professionals do to adapt to these changes and maximize their value to their employers? The International Association of Administrative Professionals (IAAP) offers seven tips:

- **Become a computer software expert.** Demonstrate your mastery of "office suite" software packages. These typically include word processing, spreadsheet, database, presentation, and scheduling software. Learn to navigate the Internet, and gather information via the Web to further your organization's goals and to serve customers' needs. Become a "Web Master" or a Web content provider for your employer.

- **Actively pursue continuing education.** Attend business-related workshops and seminars, or pursue a college degree program. Polish your written and verbal communications skills.

- **Learn how to plan conferences and meetings.** Make meetings well organized and user friendly through strong room and site selection, meeting arrangements, and audio-visuals. Understand audio and video conferencing. Become adept at presentation software such as Microsoft's PowerPoint.

- **Be a good teacher and leader.** Many administrative professionals are training and supervising other staff. The IAAP offers many opportunities to practise organizational leadership.

- **Become a communications hub for your workplace.** Clients and vendors often judge the character of a business by the quality and efficiency of its administrative support staff. Customer service skills are critically important. Interpersonal skills (tact, diplomacy, negotiation) are also essential.

- **Be an adept organizer and "Information Manager."** Utilize computerized data as well as paper office records to provide information needed by managers. Today's administrative staff increasingly conduct research and help manage projects from conception to completion.

- **Get involved in selecting and maintaining office equipment.** Stay abreast of the types of available office equipment and what is most suited to your organization. Seek out appropriate vendors. Learn to oversee equipment purchases, evaluate office supply needs, and schedule maintenance.

Source: International Association of Administrative Professionals, http://www.iaap-hq.org.

Source: riekephotos/Shutterstock

Friday

What you will practise today

> Use the skills you've developed to create and design a certificate, a fax cover sheet, and a newsletter.

> Use the special features in Microsoft Word 2007 to generate a merge.

> Compile the information you have accumulated into an agenda.

> Use Microsoft Word 2007 and your advanced skills to showcase your creative abilities to prepare a website.

You have made it to Friday. It has been a week full of new and wonderful things. Today, you can expect more of the same; it will be another busy day!

notes

8:30 A.M.

Double N's outdoor experiences have been a big success. Almost everyone who has booked one of the company's adventures has been thrilled with the whole experience. Double N is aware that word of mouth is one of the most effective methods of advertising.

Noah has been thinking of ways to help customers feel as if they have accomplished something. He wants them to go home from Double N with proof they have completed an adventure (see Figure 5.1). For some customers, this will mean overcoming a phobia; others will appreciate something tangible to remind them of the experience.

Figure 5.1
Outlook Message:
Certificates

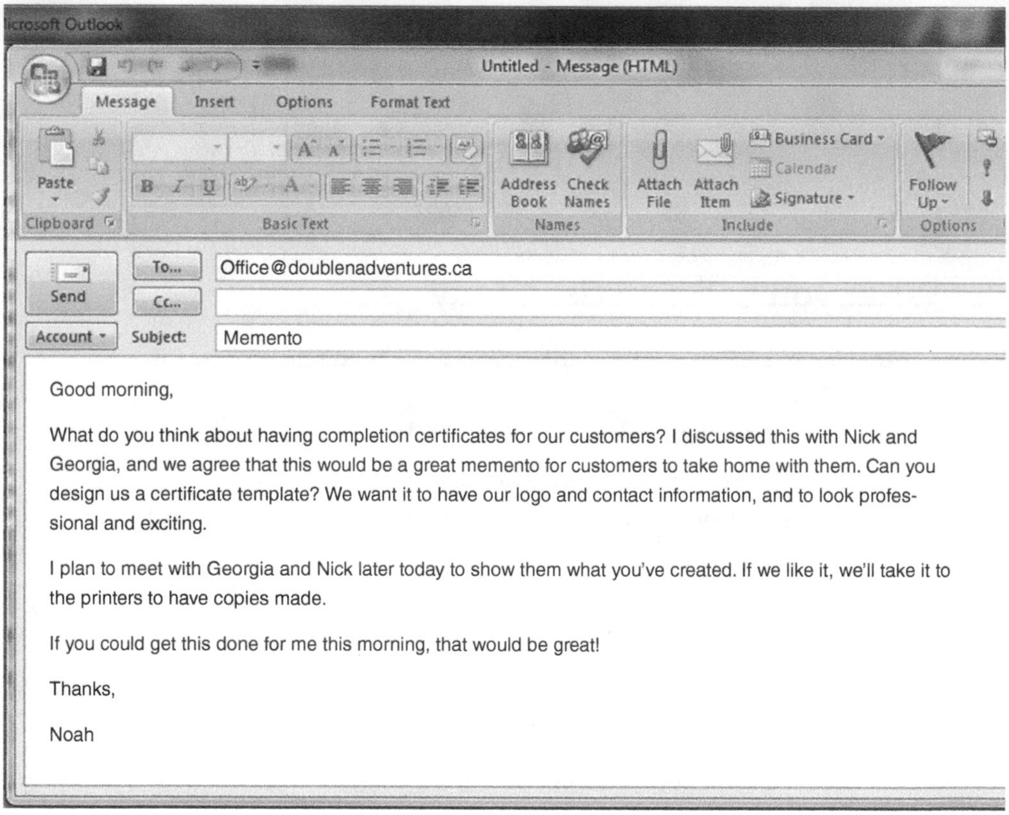

> **tip**
>
> Remember to complete the forms needed for Monday's adventure bookings. And don't forget about the weekend.

Microsoft Outlook

Untitled - Message (HTML)

Message | Insert | Options | Format Text

Paste | Clipboard | B *I* U | A | Basic Text | Address Book | Check Names | Names | Attach File | Attach Item | Signature | Business Card | Calendar | Include | Follow Up | Options

Send | To... | Office@doublenadventures.ca
Cc...
Account ▾ | Subject: | Memento

Good morning,

What do you think about having completion certificates for our customers? I discussed this with Nick and Georgia, and we agree that this would be a great memento for customers to take home with them. Can you design us a certificate template? We want it to have our logo and contact information, and to look professional and exciting.

I plan to meet with Georgia and Nick later today to show them what you've created. If we like it, we'll take it to the printers to have copies made.

If you could get this done for me this morning, that would be great!

Thanks,

Noah

Remember that you can use templates that are available online at http://office.microsoft.com/en-ca/templates/default.asp.

9:45 A.M.

Figure 5.2
Outlook Message: Invitation

Microsoft Outlook

Untitled - Message (HTML)

Message Insert Options Format Text

Paste
Clipboard

B I U   A   Basic Text

Address Check
Book Names
Names

Attach Attach
File Item
Include

Business Card
Calendar
Signature

Follow
Up
Options

Send

Account

To...   Office@doublenadventures.ca

Cc...

Subject: Trade Show Invite

Hi,

I need you to send a letter to all of our customers living in Ontario to let them know that we
will be attending the Adventures in Canada trade show next month. We want to invite them to
stop by the trade show for a visit. Let them know the dates and times of the trade show.

Merge this letter and send out to all of our Ontario customers. Don't forget to prepare the
envelopes too.

Thanks,

Georgia

10:00 A.M.

A postcard from Ralph's Extreme Pressure Washing arrived in today's mail (see Figure 5.3).

Figure 5.3
Business Postcard: Ralph's
Extreme Pressure Washing

We've Moved

Hi,
We have moved to a bigger and better location. We look
forward to seeing you at our new location. Remember, same
great people, same great business, new location!

RALPH'S
EXTREME
PRESSURE WASHING

Ralph Cheeseman
We provide on-site pressure washing for a wide
variety of items, including houses, cars, boats,
machinery, decks, etc.

141 Lakeside Drive
Corner Brook NL A1H 2L2

Phone: (709) 555-5955
Fax: (709) 555-5959
E-mail: ralph@repw.com

10:45 P.M.

Figure 5.4
Outlook Message: Fax Cover

Microsoft Outlook

Untitled - Message (HTML)

Message | Insert | Options | Format Text

Paste | Clipboard | B I U | A | Basic Text | Address Book | Check Names | Names | Attach File | Attach Item | Business Card | Calendar | Signature | Include | Follow Up | Options

Send
Account

To... | Office@doublenadventures.ca
Cc...
Subject: | Fax Cover

Hi,

Do you know what? I just noticed that we have not updated our fax cover page to match our new logo and style. Can you please create a new fax cover page template?

Thanks,

Nick

Figure 5.4
Outlook Message: Fax Cover

12:35 P.M.

Maggie Karriem just called to book a fishing adventure for seven people two weeks from Monday. She would prefer an afternoon booking. Karriem pays the deposit now by MasterCard. Her contact information is 7886 Tuscany Road NW, Calgary, AB T9B 2J8. Her phone number is (403) 292-8502.

Source: Roxane Rowsell

Every Friday you need to review the schedule and tally the number of hours worked for each adventure guide. You must e-mail the total hours for each guide to Georgia, who prepares the cheques for the guides, who pick them up at the end of the day. For the "Weekly Payroll" spreadsheet, visit the "Student Resources" link on this book's website (see Figure 5.5). The file name is weeklypayroll.xlsx. Use the following information for last Saturday and Sunday.

	Paul	Rebecca	Kelly	Tim
Saturday	Worked	Worked	Off	Off
Sunday	Worked	Worked	Worked	Off

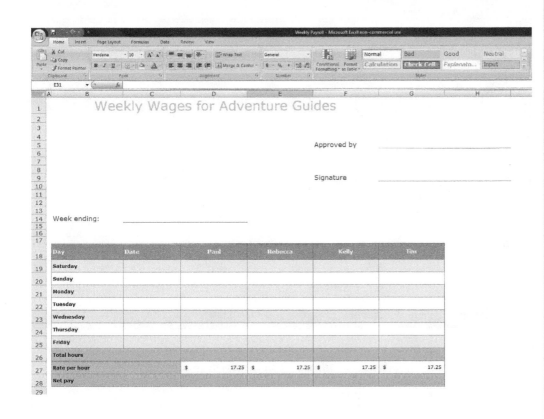

Figure 5.5
Spreadsheet: Weekly Wages for Adventure Guides

12:50 P.M.

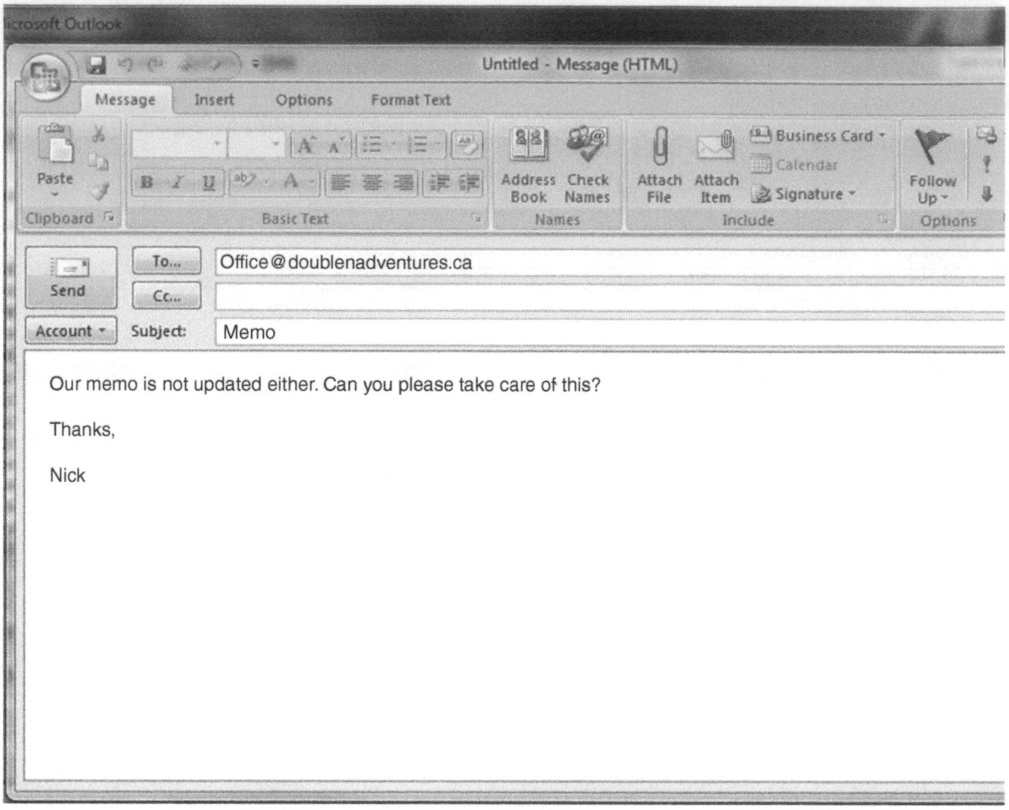

Figure 5.6
Outlook Message: Nick

To... Office@doublenadventures.ca

Cc...

Subject: Memo

Our memo is not updated either. Can you please take care of this?

Thanks,

Nick

notes

1:15 P.M.

Noah comes back from lunch smiling. He shows you a newsletter his friend just gave him. "We need a newsletter," he says. He hands you a vibrant, colourful, and professional-looking newsletter (see Figure 5.7).

Figure 5.7
Sample Newsletter

He wants you to create a two-page newsletter. Its purpose will be to inform existing clients about the company's new look, the adventures it offers, the upcoming trade show, and anything else you might think important. Noah wants it ready by the end of the day, for him to review at home over the weekend. He will then discuss it at Monday's meeting.

2:35 P.M.

Lynette White calls to book a rock climbing adventure for six people next Thursday. She pays the deposit right away by Visa. Her contact information is PO Box 873, Loon Bay, NL, A0G 1L0. Her telephone number is (709) 261-5547.

Source: Vitalii Nesterchuk/Shutterstock

Figure 5.8

Outlook Message: Contest

Photo source:
Karkas/Shutterstock

Microsoft Outlook

Untitled – Message (HTML)

| Message | Insert | Options | Format Text |

Paste | Clipboard | Basic Text | Address Book | Check Names | Names | Attach File | Attach Item | Include | Business Card | Calendar | Signature | Follow Up | Options

Send
To... | Office@doublenadventures.ca
Cc...
Account ▾ | Subject: | Contest

Noah just told me that you're designing a newsletter for us. That's great! Could you please include some information about our upcoming contest?

Here are the contest details:

We want to spur more bookings for the next 60 days. We plan to offer a booking incentive. Anyone who books an adventure with us within the next 60 days will be entered to win an exclusive Double N Adventures jacket (retail value of $150).

Include a picture of the jacket.

It would also be great if you could create a "Contest" page for our website. The draw date for the contest will be two months from today. You can create it in Word and save it as an HTML file. Our Web master will upload the file and take care of everything else.

Thanks,

Nick

Double N Adventures: A Complete Office Simulation

2:45 P.M.

That concludes the assigned jobs and tasks for today. Remember to complete all of your regular daily jobs.

Discussion Topic

All in a Day's Work

You have spent hours creating the newsletter and are quite pleased with the end result. You have just begun printing and discover that the file is too large for the memory in your printer. What will you do?

_____

_____

_____

_____

Office of the Future: 2020

The office of the future will be more mobile, with technology enabling employees to perform their jobs from almost anywhere. That is according to *Office of the Future: 2020*, a research study by OfficeTeam. The trends identified in *Office of the Future: 2005*, released in 1999, are a reality today, including the use of multi-functional, wireless technology to carry out business from various places. Also, administrative professionals are now playing a greater role in activities such as Internet research, desktop publishing, computer training and support, and website maintenance.

New Administrative Roles

The role of administrative professionals will continue to change, and careers in this field will become more complex and specialized. Many positions will require experience in specific areas such as technology, human resources, and business processes. Here are several key trends that administrative professionals can expect:

- **Entrepreneurial approach.** Administrative professionals will take an increasingly entrepreneurial approach to their jobs and careers.

- **New skill sets and responsibilities.** To advance their careers, administrative professionals will pursue business-focused training that emphasizes negotiation, delegation, budgeting, supervision, and planning skills. Other useful knowledge areas will include library science, for organizing and storing text and data used by groups; desktop publishing, for the creation of newsletters, presentation materials, and other corporate documents; and electronic communications, an emerging field concerned with ensuring the security and reliability of electronically transmitted information.

- **Specialized roles.** The administrative professional will be a specialist rather than a generalist, with job descriptions focusing on the technical and managerial aspects of day-to-day business operations.

- **Demonstrated experience.** Administrative professionals will need to show potential employers solid evidence of specialized skills and abilities, such as technical expertise and industry experience.

- **Key skills.** The most important skills and abilities for administrative professionals can be summed up with the acronym ACTION. This stands for Analysis, Collaboration, Technical aptitude, Intuition, Ongoing education, and Negotiation.

New Administrative Titles

Given the many-sided roles that administrative professionals will play in the next ten years, the title "administrative assistant," may not be enough to express the scope and depth of their skills and expertise. For this reason, new titles that reflect greater specialization will come forward. By 2020, administrative workers will likely fulfill many of the functions identified below:

- **Resource Coordinator.** Virtual offices that employ many contract workers will rely heavily on individuals who are skilled at bringing together the right human resources for a given project—much like movie producers assembling a cast, camera crew, and production team.

- **Workflow Controller.** This individual will serve as "mission control" for an organization. Whereas the resource coordinator will bring together project teams, the workflow controller will ensure that these professionals have the support and resources required to do their jobs. This position also will assist communication among teams and coordinate the transfer and use of company resources such as computers, communications equipment, and other technological tools. In smaller organizations, the same person may perform workflow control and resource coordination.

- **Knowledge Manager.** In the more fluid and project-based office of the future, this central figure will serve as a storeroom of company information, history, and best practises. They will help new employees and project professionals adapt to the organization's culture and will also perform a function similar to that of a librarian, helping people locate the documents or data necessary to perform their jobs.

- **Telecommuting Liaison.** As the number of off-site workers increases, companies will assign a telecommuter liaison to connect remote workers with one another other and with management. Individuals in this position may work with senior management to develop telecommuting policies, including helping determine which positions are suited for off-site work. Day-to-day responsibilities will include managing telecommuting schedules and providing technical support and updates to telecommuters regarding changes in operational procedures and company policies.

- **Virtual-Meetings Organizer.** This person will help employees schedule conferences and set up the necessary equipment. The virtual-meetings organizer will be technically capable and trained in the use of cameras, projection

Double N Adventures: A Complete Office Simulation

systems, electronic whiteboards, meeting software, audio equipment, and related tools.

Visit http://www.officeofthefuture2020.com to find additional research findings, survey charts, and video clips, and to test your ACTION skills.

Source: Adapted from OfficeTeam, http://www.officeofthefuture2020.com.

Source: Kelly Taylor-Hulan

Appendix A
Working Papers

The Working Papers are also available as templates at
http://www.doublenadventures.nelson.com.

Double N Adventures: A Complete Office Simulation

Block Letter

3↓ (Approximately 2" from top)

Date   2↓

Name of Recipient   Remove spacing
Company   after the address
Address
City, Province Postal Code   1↓

Dear   1↓

───
───
───
───────────────────────── 1↓

───
───────────────────────────────── 1↓

───
───
───────────────────────────────────── 1↓

───
───
───────────────────────────── 1↓

Sincerely   2↓

Your Name or Your Boss' Name   Remove Spacing 1↓
Title   1↓

xx   1↓
Enclosure: List enclosure here   1↓

c   List copy to people here

When removing space after paragraph, do not select the last line of the desired text.

If there are two or more lines for enclosure or copy notation, press Enter after each one, line up with tabs, and remove spacing after the paragraph.

Interoffice Memorandum

3⬇ (Approximately 2″ from top)

TO:	**Name of Recipient** 1⬇	
FROM:	**Your Name or Your Boss' Name** 1⬇	
DATE:	**Today's Date** 1⬇	
SUBJECT:	**An appropriate subject line** 1⬇	

_____
_____
_____
_____ 1⬇

_____
_____ 1⬇

_____
_____
_____

_____
_____
_____
_____ 1⬇

xx   1⬇

Distribution: Remove Spacing 1⬇
   First Name   Remove Spacing 1⬇
   Second Name Remove Spacing 1⬇
   Third Name

Double N Adventures: A Complete Office Simulation

Report Cover

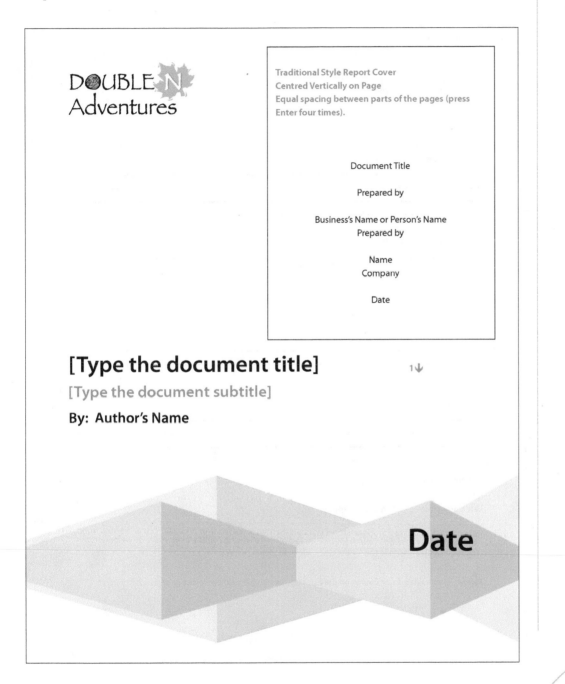

Traditional Style Report Cover
Centred Vertically on Page
Equal spacing between parts of the pages (press Enter four times).

Document Title

Prepared by

Business's Name or Person's Name
Prepared by

Name
Company

Date

[Type the document title]

1↓

[Type the document subtitle]

By: Author's Name

Date

Unbound Report

3↓ (Approximately 2" from top)

Report Title 1↓ Apply Title Style

_____

_____

_____

_____ 1↓

Side Heading 1↓ Apply Heading 1 Style

_____

_____ 1↓

☐ First bulleted point

☐ Second bulleted point

☐ Third bulleted point

_____

_____

_____

Side Heading 1↓ Apply Heading 1 Style

_____

_____

_____

_____

Left and Right Margins are set to 1" for unbound reports.

Left Margin is set to 1.5" in bound reports.

Page Numbering is traditionally in the header, positioned at the top right corner; however, in longer reports, it can be placed in the footer.

Always suppress page numbering on the first page by choosing different first page header.

Side Heading

Appendix A

Invoice

INVOICE

Would You Like An Adventure Today?

93 Red Cliff Road
Treasure Bay, NL   A9V 2K8
Phone (709) 807-4214 Fax (709) 807-4215
http://www.doublenadventures.nelson.com

INVOICE # 100
DATE:

Bill To:
Name
Company
Address
City, Province Postal Code
Phone

DESCRIPTION	NUMBER	PRICE	AMOUNT

SUBTOTAL	
HST (13%)	
GRAND TOTAL	
Minimum Deposit Required (50%)	

Make all cheques payable to Double N Adventures
If you have any questions concerning this invoice, contact [your name].

THANK YOU FOR YOUR BUSINESS!

Daily Deposit Form

DOUBLE N Adventures

Would You Like An Adventure Today?

93 Red Cliff Road
Treasure Bay, NL   A9V 2K8
Phone (709) 807-4214 Fax (709) 807-4215
http://www.doublenadventures.nelson.com

Daily Deposit

DATE:

From	Invoice #	Cash	Cheque	Credit Card
			TOTAL	
			GRAND TOTAL	

Purchase Order Form

DOUBLE N Adventures

Would You Like An Adventure Today?

Purchase Order

PLEASE SHIP TO:
93 Red Cliff Road
Treasure Bay, NL   A9V 2K8
Phone (709) 807-4214 Fax (709) 807-4215
http://www.doublenadventures.nelson.com

Purchase Order # 100
DATE:

Purchased From:
Name
Company
Address
City, Province Postal Code
Phone

DESCRIPTION	NUMBER	PRICE	AMOUNT

SUBTOTAL	
HST (13%)	
GRAND TOTAL	

Appendix B
Client Database

	A	B	C	Address
	Last Name	First Name	Company	Address
1	Last Name	First Name	Company	Address
2	Blackwood	Dana		19 Hillview T
3	Blandford	Ted		6001 Mississ
4	Budgell	Aaron	Budgituk Carving	15 Harbour \
5	Chaulk	Debbie		90 Outer Bat
6	Cheeseman	Ralph	Ralph's Extreme Pressure Washing	98 Industrial
7	Decker	Bonnie	The Two B's Bakery	65 Bottomley
8	Decker	Greg	Deckers Landscaping and Horticulture	114 Outer R(
9	Flemming	Roger		98 Red Oak [
10	George	Arch	Jack of All Trades	82 Harbourv
11	Goodyear	Jim		P.O. Box 209
12	Janson	Lydia		PO Box 63
13	Jeffery	Ronald	Laurencton Golf Club	1 Golf Club D
14	Jones	Sam		
15	Keating	Junior	Two Buddies Electrical	40 Industrial
16	Langdon	Craig		2 Flatrock Dr
17	Lawton	Derrick		115 Lincoln R
18	Lennstrom	Kim		1444 Creek !
19	Lewis	Craig		2 Flatrock Dr
20	Lewis	Len	Lewis' Ice Cream Parlor	11 Forest St
21	Ling	Connie	Open Eyes Company	
22	Luscombe	Eric	Luscombe's Welding and Fabrication	32 South Sid
23	Manual	Fred		PO Box 1567
24	Ming	Juanita		96 Mitchell S
25	Murphy	Sheila		14 Black's R(
26	Parsons	Davina		General Deliv
27	Peterson	Jason	Fit for Life Gym	PO Box 9984
28	Pico	Walace	Pico's Paving	114 Bow Cre
29	Pollerd	Hank	Pollerd's Particular Carpentry	92 Rowsell B
30	Rousel	Luke	Exploits International Airport	1 Airport Bo
31	Rowsell	Harvey		4 Edgecombe
32	Russell	Kristina		68 Melville P
33	Scott	Randy	Anytime Pressure Washing	43 Larch Str
34	Senger	Rob	Rob's Auto Detailing	52 Lakeside [
35	Sheppard	Dennis	Nature's Best Greenery	23 Chester C
36	Simms	Georgia		54 Green Hill
37	Snow	Susan		PO Box 17
38	Strowbridge	Tim		13 Elm Stree
39	Sutton	Andrew		98 Carrick D
40	Tayler	William		4 Birch Stree
41	Wells	Derrick		P.O. Box 42
42	West	James		P.O. Box 390
43	White	Kerry	The Candy Barn	
44	Young	Ben	Young's Trucking	112 Outer R(
45	Wells	Richard	Well's Fishing	56 Main Stre
46				
47				
48				

Sheet1 | Sheet2 | Sheet3